TO THINK WITHOUT FEAR

THE CHALLENGE OF THE EXTRA-TERRESTRIAL

ANTHONY DUNCAN

SKYLIGHT PRESS

© The estate of Anthony Duncan, 2015

First published in Great Britain in 2015 by Skylight Press,
210 Brooklyn Road, Cheltenham, Glos GL51 8EA

All rights reserved. Except for the quotation of short passages for the purposes of criticism and review, no part of this publication may be reproduced, stored in a retrieval system or transmitted, in any form or by any means, electronic, mechanical, photocopying, recording or otherwise, without the prior consent of the copyright holder and publisher.

Anthony Duncan has asserted his right to be identified as the author of this work.

Designed and typeset by Rebsie Fairholm
Selections edited by Gareth Knight
Publisher: Daniel Staniforth
Cover design and photography by Rebsie Fairholm incorporating stock texture from sirius-sdz.deviantart.com

www.skylightpress.co.uk

Printed and bound in Great Britain by Lightning Source, Milton Keynes.
Typeset in Agmena Pro. Titles set in Sursum.

British Library Cataloguing in Publication Data:
A catalogue record for this book is available from the British Library.

ISBN 978-1-908011-63-3

CONTENTS

PART ONE: *Daring to Think the Unthinkable, and coming to terms with its implications.*

Prologue		7
Chapter One	The Merits of Conditioning	9
	The Limitations of Conditioning	10
	Conditioning and Dogmatism	11
	Maturity: Three Objectives	12
	Liberation from Fear	14
	Processes of the Eternal Mind	14
	Thinking Without Fear	15
Chapter Two	Encounters with the Otherworldly	17
	Beginning to Think the Unthinkable	19
	Challenging the World-Views	20
	Psychology – Which Way?	21
Chapter Three	A Challenge to Religion?	23
	Our Separated Brethren?	25
	Seeing Ourselves?	27
	A Disturbing Possibility?	28
Chapter Four	The Third Discipline	31
	Muddy Waters?	32
	Looking in the Wrong Direction	33
	The Essential Blessedness of Nature	34
	Nature and Grace	35
	A Doctrine of Re-Creation	37
Chapter Five	Concerning Heaven	40
	The Image of God	41
	Transfiguration and Absorption	42
	Provisional Conclusions	43

PART TWO: *Making Sense of the Impossible. A Necessary Riot of Speculations.*

Prologue to Part Two		47
Chapter Six	Human and Humanoid	49
	Where Do They Come From?	50
	A Preferred Alternative	51
	Complicating the Universe?	52
	Come Back, Gallileo, All is Forgiven!	53
	The Insights of Religion	53
Chapter Seven	Atmosphere, or Aura?	56
	Concerning the Earth's Aura	57
	Why Do They Come at All?	58
	A Recapitulation	60
Chapter Eight	Trial And Error: Extra-Terrestrial Evolution?	62
	Speculation, and More Speculation!	64
	A Highly Unfashionable View	65
Chapter Nine	Dependence Upon Externals	67
	Conceptions of Time and Space	68
	Unfashionable Evidence to Hand	68
	Recapitulation	71
Chapter Ten	Alternative Universes	72

PART THREE: *An Exercise in Absurdity: A Thought Thinks the Mind.*

Prologue To Part Three		77
Chapter Eleven	Living By Metaphor	79
	The Creation of Worlds and their Creatures	79
	A Matter of Scale	80
	Not Cosmology but Creativity	82
	Creation Re-Launched	82
Chapter Twelve	All Creatures Modify Each Other	85
	The Lord of the Dance	87
Chapter Thirteen	Coordinates and Bridging the Dimensional Gaps	92
	Meetings of Minds	94
	What Are We Doing Here?	95
Chapter Fourteen	Folk Memory	96
	The Sense of Alienation	97
	The Effects of Alienation	99
	An Inhuman Condition	100
Chapter Fifteen	The Avatara	102
	The Archetypal Image	103
	The Anointed One	103
	The Incarnation	104
	The Cosmic Implications	105

PART FOUR: *Daring to Guess the Unguessable. The Quest for New Creation?*

Prologue to Part Four		111
Chapter Sixteen	Mind-to-Mind Communication	113
	The Linking of Minds and Mind-Systems	115
	Searching the Memories	117
Chapter Seventeen	Growth Towards an End-Product	121
	Enlarging Our Vision of Things	122
Chapter Eighteen	Keeping Our Heads Above the Water	124
	A Terminological Quest	126
	The Sound of One Hand, Clapping	127
Chapter Nineteen	A Manner of Seeing and Not Seeing	128
	Paradox and Perplexity	129
Chapter Twenty	Postscript	133

Appendix A
The Liberation of the Imagination: an essay

Part One: Concerning the Imagination	141
Part Two: "Tae See Oorsels As Ithers See Us"	159
Part Three: The Practical Use of a Balanced Spirituality	172
Part Four: Imagine, If You Can, Once Again	179

Appendix B
Educational Experiences 187

1. Of an Alternative Universe?	187
2. From Elsewhere Within This Universe?	196
3. A Mutual Attempt at Communication	198

PART ONE

Daring to Think the Unthinkable, and coming to terms with its implications

PROLOGUE

THERE is a category, among the canonised Saints of the Christian East, which is known as "The Fool in Christ." Perhaps their own patron was the great St Paul, who was once told by a Very Important Person that he was out of his mind; his much learning had driven him mad. Beyond St Paul, however, there stands the Incarnate Son of God, who was without doubt the most remarkable anti-hero in the history of mankind; the Fool Himself and none other.

Wise or foolish, clever or stupid, there is only one thing that I care about and that is that I am, and shall forever be, *in Christ*. What the wise and the clever regard as folly, therefore, is unimportant. Each man and woman has his, or her, own calling; if mine is to be a fool, then let me be, in however small the print, *a fool in Christ*.

Needless to say, it is easier by far to be a fool when one's age is nearer seventy than twenty and, in this connection, the date of the commencement of this work – the First of April, or All Fools' Day – is delightfully appropriate. It is appropriate in that I am called, in my foolishness, to cross the sacred boundaries of irreconcilable categories of thought, to confuse any number of well-established and respectably exclusive disciplines, and to attempt to paint upon a much wider canvas than is normal.

I confess that it is daunting to contemplate, in addition, the undoubted fact that the canvas in question is poly-dimensional as well as being far too wide for comfort. The task must be attempted, however, and only a fool can be expected to attempt it, for fools are very slightly less subject to the massive conditionings of attitude and thought – characteristic of our mortal, human condition – than the clever and the wise. They are certainly less subject than those of the clever and the wise who, additionally, suffer the misfortune of being thought respectable.

What, therefore, provokes this exercise in foolishness, and what is the nature of it? As the profounder truths can only find verbal expression in poetry, I can but offer a poetic answer. For I am challenged by an encounter – nay more, by a friendship. I find myself challenged by a new-found friend to think, and to think afresh and more widely than I have ever thought before. Answering this challenge is, for me, a matter of personal and professional integrity.

> *We do not share the same biology*
> *my friend; for oxygen, and food, and drink*
> *do not sustain or limit you, I think.*
> *Your life is lived by other energy.*
> *Two persons of one creature, you and me;*
> *our friendship makes the Universe to shrink*
> *and brings our worldly wisdom to the brink.*
> *Our world-views fail, and our theology.*
>
> *They fail for both conditioned are, and small;*
> *respectable, parameters secure,*
> *a cosyness for learned men's careers.*
> *Our friendship makes a nonsense of it all,*
> *blows through a breath of air, both fresh and pure.*
> *Affection and respect transcend all fears.*

CHAPTER ONE

I AM massively conditioned in what I think, in what I expect, and in what I take for granted. This is neither surprising nor is it necessarily undesirable for I was born, not into a vacuum, but into a context. I was born, indeed, into an interwoven pattern of contexts; racial, social, temporal – in that I was born in the 20th century and not the 19th – religious, political and other. I went to school; indeed I went to a number of schools as my parents moved house frequently in response to the demands of my Father's job. And then I served, first as an officer in the Army, and then, for well over thirty years, as a parish clergyman.

Add up all the possibilities of conditioning, in thought, expectations and attitudes, that nearly seventy years of this can produce and it could seem formidable indeed, if not actually insurmountable. Formidable it certainly was; insurmountable it is certainly not, for maturity and true inner growth are substantially to do with growing out of one's conditionings, transcending them and emerging free of them. But they are no less to do with retaining a proper respect and a true compassion for this veritable chrysalis of conditionings from which the butterfly has joyfully emerged.

THE MERITS OF CONDITIONING

Conditioning is, in any event, a convenience; it provides useful everyday parameters to a man's, or a woman's earthly life. I am presently sitting at a wooden table. It responds to furniture polish and at the same time it is vulnerable to saws, hammers, the claws of large dogs, the attentions of small children, and abrasives in general. It is good, and it is certainly extremely convenient, to be able to accept everyday things at their face value.

If, however, I habitually thought of my dining-table as a complex molecular structure which, if examined in sufficient depth, must dissolve into a microcosmic universe of atoms, sub-atomic particles and the rest (some of which are capable of giving the impression that they move backwards in time as well as forwards), all of which is held in coherent being only by an unfathomable intention proceeding from the depths of The Mystery – I should never get round to laying it for luncheon!

The fact remains, however, that both approaches to my dining-table are at once valid and are of equal importance. I emphasise – *they are of equal importance.*

My conditioning causes me to accept the Earth and its Moon, the Solar System and all that we know of the Universe, at their current face value. This face value is in a perpetual state of flux, however, due to the steady advances that are made in scientific knowledge. Nevertheless, though our understanding of them deepens, they remain what they are, or rather, they remain *what to us they seem to be.*

I am encouraged to rejoice in what might, perhaps, turn out to be signs of the possibility of organic life on the planet Mars, and also upon certain of the moons which circle the planet Jupiter. There is an evident yearning in many of the scientific community to make the discovery that, after all, we on Earth are not entirely alone in an otherwise lifeless – and thus essentially meaningless – Universe.

THE LIMITATIONS OF CONDITIONING

I am, however, conditioned to respect the boundaries of the various human disciplines. When thinking in terms of science and of its various discoveries, I must think scientifically and in scientific terms. When contemplating essentially religious insights and understandings, I must think religiously and in religious terms. My mind is thus positively encouraged – if not actually constrained – to function in, and out of, a collection of watertight boxes. It must be admitted that there are advantages in this and that the disciplines thus imposed are, in the main, positive and helpful.

My conditioning also causes me to take for granted that all life, and in particular, human life, is – and indeed must be – biologically based and that no other possibility can reasonably be expected. The chemical basis of life, from which we can understand the biological to have evolved, is the only one of which we have the slightest scientific experience. I may very well be inwardly persuaded that I am more – and other – than a perambulating chemistry set, but my conditioning discourages me from taking this into serious consideration when thinking scientifically, and thus in purely scientific terms.

By the same token, my conditioning causes me to ride roughshod over any number of specifically scientific considerations when I am thinking religiously!

I am conditioned, perhaps most subtly of all, by the language I was brought up to speak and which is thus the vehicle for the expression of my thoughts. Thoughts require articulation and they are thus, to some extent at least, moulded and channelled by the means of articulation available.

The English language is, fortunately, capable of a formidable precision as well as a wealth of poetic expression. To an extent which is almost certainly greater than I realise, I am both enabled and limited by it. The language I speak undoubtedly influences the way I think.

What matters, however, is that I become aware of the reality of these manifold – and mostly good – conditioning agencies and their effects upon me. And then what matters most is that, being thus aware, *I do not reject any of them but learn to transcend them altogether*. This is important, for outright rejection of one's own conditioning is a rejection both of heritage and of culture. It results, as often as not, in a self-conscious identification with another culture, quite foreign to one's own, for men and women live neither in splendid isolation nor in a vacuum. This, in its turn, is usually accompanied by a headlong and uncritical plunge into a quite foreign pattern of conditionings in the fond belief that this constitutes some kind of "liberation." Few are genuinely edified thereby, and even fewer are actually "liberated."

CONDITIONING AND DOGMATISM

Conditioning and dogmatism tend to walk hand-in-hand. Dogmatism is, as often as not, a symptom either of intellectual idleness or of unacknowledged fear. Dogmatism digs deep trenches and erects broad entanglements of barbed wire in front of them. Dogmatism encases itself in concrete, peers through its periscopes and weapon-slits, and prepares to resist all assaults upon its cherished positions to the very bitter end.

To the entrenched dogmatic, everyone who is not in the same bunker can very easily seem to be either a heretic or an enemy. The bunkers themselves can be made extremely cosy; they can be lavishly – even tastefully – decorated, and there is often a great camaraderie among those within them. It has also to be acknowledged that, in the total scheme of things within the human condition, they have their right and proper place.

Religion is littered with defensive works of this nature. Sometimes, and particularly in times of great trial, they are urgently needed. But defensive works, of various degrees of complexity, are to be encountered in every field of human learning, and in most other fields of human activity as well. The defensive bunker is not therefore to be entirely deplored, negative though its influence can often be, for it is the very trench-system out of which great numbers of brave men and women have climbed in order to walk forward, in Faith and great courage, into the unknown. They have found themselves equipped to face all the dangers ahead of them by their faithful preparation and training in the particular bunker that has nurtured them.

In ordinary, mortal human conflict, wars are not won by the combatants sitting in defensive positions but by climbing out of them, taking the ground ahead, holding it and continuing the advance. The whole process of human maturity proceeds in much the same way but it is possibly understood more clearly by contrasting its three principal objectives.

MATURITY: THREE OBJECTIVES

The first objective is the attainment of *Knowledge*. Knowledge is associated with capability, even with power. "I know, therefore I can!" It can, needless to say, easily induce a massive inflation of the Ego. "I know more than you, therefore I am superior to you!" The acquisition of knowledge, at all levels, on all fronts and in all departments of life, is an integral part of human growth, both social and individual, and it proceeds – as it must – for as long as earthly life is lived. When an individual no longer has the desire to learn, he or she is already as good as dead!

Knowledge, as an end in itself, however, is purposeless. It is possible for anyone to become, in the well-known expression, "a mine of useless information." Knowledge, deprived of purpose, can be both useless and dangerous. A malicious mind can do immense harm, both to itself and to others, given the necessary knowledge. An immature and irresponsible mind can do just as much damage without the slightest malicious intent.

It is necessary, therefore, that there be a clear intention behind the quest *to know*. "I seek to know in order to serve," is an admirable statement of intent, for every kind of knowledge, and at every kind of level, brings its own related responsibilities with it.

It is, however, hardly necessary to add that my Ego must be kept firmly in check if it is not to enthrone itself as a little "god" within me, just because I may, perchance, have acquired a store of knowledge in some field or other which my neighbour, or neighbours seem to lack!

Knowledge is on one level; *Understanding*, the second objective, is on another, and higher, level altogether. Understanding both contains knowledge and transcends it. It is of the nature of understanding that *it understands*; it perceives what it is that a particular field of which knowledge is sought is all about. Understanding perceives how things really work and why they are as they are. In terms of the conflicts between individuals and societies it has wisely been observed that "to understand is to forgive." To understand is to perceive that practically nothing is ever what its face value might suggest it to be; there are always depths both behind and within things which are not accessible to knowledge on its own.

Understanding and compassion go hand-in-hand. There is no Ego-inflation in true understanding for, unlike knowledge which is inward-looking in that, essentially, it seeks *to get*, understanding is outward-looking in that, essentially, it seeks *to give*. Knowledge and understanding represent two fundamental steps in human maturity, and the step up, from the one to the other, is a moral and spiritual advance of no small order.

The third objective, *Wisdom*, both contains Understanding and transcends it altogether. Wisdom and compassion are inextricably interwoven and wisdom manifests the perfect balance of those apparent opposites, detachment and involvement. Wisdom is completely detached and, at the same time, is completely involved. There is no longer a shred of that immature counterfeit of detachment and involvement which we know as "identification." In wisdom there is no identification whatsoever either of self with endeavour, or of endeavour with self.

Wisdom is supremely confident of ultimate outcomes, for wisdom itself belongs to *the Ultimate*; it proceeds from the very heart of The Mystery.

LIBERATION FROM FEAR

What has here been outlined is *a Way*. It is a way of transcendence, transcending both conditioning and the variously motivated searchings for knowledge. It leads towards *a state of abiding* in the "all shall be well, and all shall be well, and all manner of thing shall be well" which the mystic Julian of Norwich heard from the lips of Christ. By the same token, it is an abiding in the stated Truth that all that exists, is, and shall ever be, "forasmuch as God loveth it."

The process is one of liberation from fear into a freedom both to become, and to think. A wise man once said, somewhere, that "the third-rate mind is only happy when it is thinking with the majority; the second-rate mind is only happy when it is thinking with the minority, and the first-rate mind is only happy when it is thinking!" I am unsure of the original context of this remark. It may once have referred to an academic assessment of scholarly minds but its truth is far more profound than this. There is a sense in which it seems almost to run parallel to the progression: Knowledge, Understanding, Wisdom, but this parallel is only valid in so far as it indicates *a calling*, for, in Christ, the calling of every man and woman is *to think without fear*. This is the real criterion of first-rateness, not academic or intellectual ability.

To think without fear is to occupy a position from which the mind can be led into an ever more profound participation in Mind Itself. This is the quest, not for Knowledge, or even for Understanding, but for Wisdom. Wisdom carries with it a sublime and all-transcending contentment, not necessarily to know, nor even necessarily to understand, but to accept joyfully, with an unconditional love.

When a person is liberated from a sometimes obsessional desire to know and to understand, and indeed while that person is in the way of liberation and has come to recognize it for what it is, then a whole new world of possibilities begins to open wide. We are concerned with Mind. The Buddhist insistence that "all is Mind" gives an insight, to those who will permit it, into both our circumstances and our difficulties.

PROCESSES OF THE ETERNAL MIND

Our circumstances may be summed up very briefly. I suggest that we are all "thoughts in the Mind of God." The Christian insistence that "all things are in God and God is in all things" preserves us from falling into a full-blooded transcendentalism on the one hand, or a full-blooded immanentism on the other. There is, nevertheless, an innate transcendentalist tendency in a great many Christians which needs to be brought into balance by what we might possibly describe as "the pantheist experience." But the Christian orthodoxy of *Pantheism* is a statement of that necessary equilibrium: "All things are in God and God is in all things."

The Kalahari Bushmen have, perhaps, the most poetically stated, and arguably the most faithful doctrine of all. "There is a Dream dreaming us." They are, however, far too sensible, and too close to reality, pompously to define it as a doctrine!

We use the word "God" because we have none other. It is, however, but a label for us to tie on No-Thing. We are referring to *The Mystery*. Of The Mystery it has rightly been said that its *essence* is unknowable and utterly unfathomable. It is known by, and through, its *energies*. We are in no position to distinguish between the Dreamer and the Dream, though such a distinction is faithful to our own experience of life and it is thus a faithful distinction for us to make in principle.

Creation, I therefore suggest, represents the contents of a Mind. Creatures, at all levels of their being, are the thoughts and imaginings of that Mind and might be expected to reflect its character. We ourselves are thoughts in that same Mind and are thus made of Mind-stuff. Our own created minds participate in the workings of Mind to the limits of their creaturely capacity but, I also suggest, it is beyond the capacity of a thought to objectify and define its Thinker.

The Mystery, in whose Mind all that exists is the sum of its thoughts, defies all our nearly obsessional attempts to fit a front door and a back door to its unfathomable Abyss.

THINKING WITHOUT FEAR

Freedom to think without fear releases the thinker into an acceptance of the hitherto impossible. As his Ego no longer needs to be able to know and to understand any and every experience or encounter, he is able both to take things as he finds them and to accept creatures as they are. He is also able to relate to phenomena by means of metaphor, when all other means fail him. Radio and television supply him with an ample stock of possible metaphors by which he can relate to the possibility of life existing on wavelengths other than his own, and thus presently both inaccessible to his perceptions and beyond the possibilities of his technology.

He is also released from the absolute necessity of taking himself and his own mode of being as the unalterable and eternal criterion. It becomes possible, therefore, to accept – if not yet to understand – the possibility of a human-like person existing upon another, but close, wavelength, whose physical expression or mode of being is *other than biological* in the earthly sense. He is released into the possibility of communication with such a person, without having to know or to understand every detail of its operation. He is able to take things as he finds them.

Having been freed from fear, he is also released into the possibility of a person-to-person relationship developing which is based in the first instance upon mutual acceptance and trust, and thereafter upon the mutual affection and respect which permits an ever-deepening meeting of two minds. The two minds are discovered to be very close and very similar, but to differ considerably in experience. But why are either parties surprised? Both minds are creations of, and partakers in, *the Mind of The Mystery* which has thought them both.

CHAPTER TWO

A CQUAINTANCE with brethren who are not in this world as we are in this world is a normal human experience. It is conducted for the most part, however, beyond the boundaries of an individual's normal field of consciousness. It is therefore entirely possible for one who, for whatever reason, has difficulties in accepting the existence of angels, to be on the most intimate terms – at a deeper level of his mind – with his holy guardian angel! The accidents of human, earthly life, the imbalance between the twin faculties of reason and intuition within an individual, and the grand intellectual arguments in support of this stance, or that, affect the underlying realities not at all.

ENCOUNTERS WITH THE ☉THERWORLDLY

Our encounters on the threshold of consciousness, or just beyond its normal bounds, are mostly Earth-related. Those whose psychic perceptions are highly active are seldom surprised by the occasional encounter with others who are in what we may best describe as a post-mortem state. Sometimes these encounters are morbid and disagreeable, sometimes not. This whole field of experience and concern, however, need not detain us now. Others, from time to time, are made aware in various ways of the vibrant reality of what the Church describes as The Communion of Saints. This, rightly understood, is the eternal fellowship of all those who are in Christ, their fellowship transcending the boundaries of mortal Earthly life altogether. Encounters of this sort are usually very Earth-related but not in the slightest degree Earth-bound, as the categories referred to earlier frequently seem to be.

The reality of the "inner guide" is very apparent to some individuals. These "inner guides" sometimes give the impression that they are parts of the total personality of that individual, but sometimes they seem to be quite external to it. It is also occasionally perceived that inner guidance operates upon more than one level.

There is, in addition to all these possible "fields of encounter," that which transcends them all, unmistakably and absolutely. This is an encounter at what is usually described as being at a mystical level, and it is with Heaven itself in some form or another.

There can be nothing essentially unusual or untoward, therefore, in our encounter with another consciousness which does not find its material expression in biological terms and whose vitality does not therefore depend upon eating, drinking or oxygen to keep its biological machine from grinding to a terminal halt.

There are, needless to say, multitudes of good, honest and intelligent men and women who would deny out of hand the reality of any of the encounters hitherto mentioned. It would be claimed that they are all, in various ways, the product of an over-suggestive imagination, or that they have psychological – even pathological – origins and explanations. With such good folk I must disagree and hope that it is possible to "agree to differ" with mutual respect.

Certain it is that the intuitive perceptions – call them "psychic" if you must – are naturally active and developed in some people, whereas they appear to be substantially dormant in others. I recall an argument, almost a heated argument, between two clerics, both of them academically well qualified. It concerned the objective reality and actual existence of angels. The one denied their actual existence, the other decidedly affirmed it. The one cried; "with your degree and your academic background you *can't possibly* believe in the actual existence of angels!" The other, with equal passion, responded; "Good heavens, man! Don't you *know!*"

Here we have the communications impasse in a nutshell. It arises, I suggest, not only in the difference between individuals' sensitivities and their degree of activation, but also from the radical imbalance, in Western culture in particular, between the twin faculties of reason and intuition within the individual. In Western culture, and most particularly in Protestant Western culture, reason is exalted and intuition is discounted, often virtually denied, and sometimes it is even demonised! Our differing clerics represent the near-impossibility of *communicating experience* to one who has not experienced, and thus has no conception of what it is so to experience. The latter cannot, yet, fit the idea of such an experience into his or her scheme of things – his or her world-view. And a man will often be tempted to kill in defence of his world view!

BEGINNING TO THINK THE UNTHINKABLE

I may have already begun to part company with some intending readers. Some may have gone! To those that remain, I respectfully suggest that they follow me a little further, if they dare, for I make no claim to be other than a fool; so long as I may be, and remain, *a fool-in-Christ*.

Having established my preferred credentials, I am bound to justify them straight away by introducing a subject which is all but unmentionable in the context of any of our respectable conditionings, and is able only to be contemplated, if at all, in a water-tight, semi-fictional box of its very own. I refer, of course, to that phenomenon generally known as the "Unidentified Flying Object" or, more popularly, as "The Flying Saucer."

This phenomenon carries with it something of a blessing in that it throws all our learned disciplines into an equal measure of disarray. It challenges every respectable world-view and is, needless to say, the subject both of silly, official "cover-ups" and of the consequent – and increasingly threadbare – "disinformation" campaigns that accompany such activities.

We are bound, sooner or later nevertheless, to ask ourselves at least a minimal number of the questions these phenomena suggest.

What is this that appears, and disappears, both from our sight and from our radar screens and appears to defy all known laws of flight and aerodynamics?

What is this that defies our present knowledge of astronomy, of physics, of astrophysics and all the rest? Where do these things come from, and how, and why do they come at all?

What is this that, by its very nature, must constitute a challenge to religious insight and theological thought of every kind? What might its relevance be, in the context of such insights as we have? Why is this challenge unheeded and why does the theological mind remain firmly and comfortably buried, ostrich-like, in the sand?

What of the ever-growing multitude of reported encounters with human-like, or humanoid, beings connected with these U.F.Os? What of the considerable number of reported abductions and return, of men, women and children? What of their examinations by curious and evidently interested – but essentially benevolent – humanoids, clearly anxious not to cause harm?

CHALLENGING THE WORLD-VIEWS

Our world-views are challenged and, as a consequence, the challenge is either ignored or denied. We retreat into compartmental thinking and, at best, give this kind of experience a watertight compartment of its own. Witnesses are usually said to have been the victims of hallucination, suggestion – almost anything as long as they don't have to be taken *threateningly seriously*. Seldom does "the scientific" reveal itself as being so subjective and essentially unscientific as – in some at least – of its dealings with those who claim encounter with *persons who would appear to be extra-terrestrial*.

Our world-views are formed by our conditionings. There is no greater threat to a man's equilibrium than a sudden and radical challenge to his world-view. But if, as I suggest, the response by some parts at least of the world of science has been somewhat less than scientific, what of the response by the trusted and responsible custodians of Religious Faith? I suggest that no more urgent, or exciting, challenge – or stimulation – to our understandings of Revealed Truth has made its appearance in two thousand years.

It is probably true to say that the scientific world will not feel completely at ease with the idea of Unidentified Flying Objects, and even less with their possible crews, until there is both wreckage to analyse and corpses to dissect. In all fairness it must be acknowledged that science has to do, essentially, with *the mechanics of things*, however exalted or sophisticated those mechanics might be. Science is concerned with the question "how?" The question "why?" is outside its brief.

Religion, however, is essentially to do with the question "why?" It has to do with the dynamics of things on the highest of levels, that of *meaning*. It has to do, first of all, with the relationships between creatures and their Origin, and between the creatures themselves as a consequence of that primary relationship. In the pursuit of these concerns it is accustomed to think, and to reach, beyond the bounds of mortal earthly life, and it does so in two directions.

Here, perhaps, lies the source of a difficulty, for the present challenge is to reach out *in a third direction*. The "reachings beyond" by religion in its various forms have either been a "reaching up" by the higher religions, in the direction of Heaven, or a "reaching down", usually by the less developed religious traditions, in the direction of the underworld as it is variously perceived. The present challenge is *to reach across*, to relate face to face, and to discover meaning in the encounter *for both parties*. For creation is a unity and all minds partake of Mind Itself, in the measure appropriate for them.

Perhaps it is time to pause in our headlong rush into what many will regard as madness. I have taken for granted, so far, the objective reality of the Unidentified Flying Object. I have also accepted, so far, that there appear to be conscious minds involved in them and in their operation. I have therefore made the assumption that they are vehicles of a sort and that they have crews within them. I have accepted, in principle at least, the testimony of a growing multitude concerning encounters with "other" and seemingly Extra-Terrestrial persons who have generally given the impression of being both purposeful and essentially harmless, even benevolent.

PSYCHOLOGY – WHICH WAY?

For centuries, and most decidedly since the beginning of this century, writers and visionaries have speculated about space travel. As more and more of Planet Earth has yielded its secrets to mankind, so his restless spirit of adventure has driven him to seek new frontiers. I suggest that there may be only two new frontiers which are open to him to explore. The first of these is his own subconscious mind. The emergence of such prophetic figures as Freud and Jung and the consequent explosion of psychological interest and awareness, together with a not unrelated fascination with matters of esoteric and occult lore, are evidence enough of the vigour with which this hitherto unsuspected frontier is being explored, though not always wisely.

The second frontier is represented by the Solar System and Outer Space. Man has walked on the Moon, unmanned probes have penetrated almost to the limits of the Solar System and the mysteries uncovered so far pose more questions than the answers they supply. There is an almost desperate desire to find evidence of organic life, dead, alive or latent, *somewhere else*. The idea that mankind is alone in a dead Universe, though fashionable among the sceptical, is somehow intolerable at a level much deeper than fashionable scepticism.

A product of the exploration of both these frontiers is the veritable explosion of Science Fiction during the last half-century. "Outer Space" versions of the old "Cops and Robbers" or "Cowboy and Indian" stories abound, and most profitably both to their writers and to their publishers. The "Good Guys" – ourselves, are in perpetual righteous mortal conflict with the "Bad Guys" – the others. All this is, needless to say, the expression, in a new fictional genre, of mortal man's innate imbalance and self-destructive paranoia.

This same paranoia, projected into Outer Space, results in fighter aircraft being vectored to intercept U.F.Os appearing and disappearing on Air Defence radar screens. And the possible military potential of U.F.O. technology exercises a great many, officially sceptical, minds all over the globe. Nothing is more important than for a nation state to be a step or two ahead in the business of mass-murder and wholesale destruction!

The question which is raised, however, and which must be honestly faced, is quite fundamental. Is this explosion of U.F.O. interest, claims of sightings, encounters with Extra-Terrestrial beings and so on, a manifestation of some almost global psychological aberration; the product of massive suggestion on susceptible minds? Or do we turn this possibility on its head and detect – in our own yearnings and the pushings of our own frontiers, psychologically, in aerospace technology and in the new mythologies of Science Fiction – an essentially unconscious, across-the-board response to a fundamental dynamic at the very heart of things? A fundamental dynamic, moreover, to which the U.F.O. and its intelligences may also be responding in their ventures into our aura, our airspace and our consciousness?

Some will, in all honesty and good faith, choose the first answer. Others, with equal integrity, will chose the second, and it will by now have become apparent that I am one of the latter. Regardless of which stance is taken, however, it is before all else necessary that the individual is liberated from all compulsion, either to think with the majority or to think with the minority. He or she must be free *to think without fear*.

CHAPTER THREE

I HAVE introduced what I believe to be a fundamental challenge, both to our scientific and to our religious world-views. I suggest that what may be described as the outward and visible sign of this challenge – the Unidentified Flying Object as it is both seen by the eye and recorded upon radar screens, together with the persons associated with it who, when encountered, are perceived as being both similar to ourselves and also dissimilar – may very well prove, one day, to have somewhat resembled the tip of an iceberg. The depths are yet to be consciously encountered. Be that as it may, the phenomenon is unlikely to go away and, sooner or later, the questions it poses will have to be addressed. It is of the first importance that they be addressed, from the outset, without fear.

A CHALLENGE TO RELIGION?

We mortal men and women, here upon this earth, are to all intents and purposes totally conditioned into interpreting our deepest insights and experiences exclusively in terms of ourselves and our own circumstances. The whole apparatus of religion is, I suggest, an essentially Earthly – even worldly – phenomenon. It represents both *a search for meaning*, and also *an awareness of loss* and of dis-order, variously perceived, which makes the search for meaning necessary in the first place.

The Christian Revelation is one of Incarnation. In the words of the Fourth Gospel:

In the beginning was the Word;
the Word was with God
and the Word was God...

The Word was made flesh,
he lived among us,

> *and we saw his glory,*
> *the glory that is his as the only Son of the Father,*
> *full of grace and truth.*
> (Jn 1: 1 & 14)

This is no academic or theological proposition for "we saw his glory." And, from the same writer, we are told:

> *Something which has existed since the beginning,*
> *that we have heard,*
> *and we have seen with our own eyes;*
> *that we have watched*
> *and touched with our hands;*
> *the Word, who is life —*
> *this is our subject.*
> *That life was made visible;*
> *we saw it and we are giving our testimony ...*
> (Jn 1: 1 & 2)

That to which St John gives the name "The Word" is best understood as the creative and creating principle at the very heart of The Mystery whom we call God. In the poetry of Christian doctrine, "The Word" is the Second Person of the Holy and Indivisible Trinity, three Persons and one God.

Belief in the Incarnation is simply enough stated. To come to terms with its implications, however, is a task practically beyond the human mental process altogether. It is not surprising, therefore, that there has always existed a tendency among Christians, both clerical and lay, to cut the Mystery of the Incarnation down to a more manageable size; to reduce the mysteries of its Mystery to human proportions by dwelling upon one facet of it at a time. Thus the Nativity, the Passion, the Resurrection, the Ascension and the Re-creation heralded by the Pentecost experience, are treated, liturgically, one after the other as if they were actually separable.

The Mystery of the Incarnation, however, is a unity. Its significance was understood, at a very early stage in the life of the Christian Church, to be Cosmic, Universal, Eternal.

> *In the beginning was the Word*
> *the word was with God*
> *and the Word was God.*
> *He was with God in the beginning.*
> *Through him all things came to be,*
> *not one thing had its being but through him …*
>
> *and he was coming into the world.*
> *He was in the world*
> *that had its being through him …*
> *(Jn 1: 1-3 & 9-10)*

> *He is the image of the unseen God*
> *and the first-born of all creation,*
> *for in him were created*
> *all things in heaven and on earth;*
> *everything visible and everything invisible …*
> *all things were created through him and for him,*
> *before any thing was created, he existed,*
> *and he holds all things in unity …*
>
> *… he is the Beginning.*
> *(Col 1: 15-17)*

The Cosmic and Eternal and the intimately domestic and personal are completely inseparable, however difficult it can be to hold the two together within our understanding at the same time.

OUR SEPARATED BRETHREN?

The challenge posed to our religious insights by the U.F.O. and its crew is not a challenge to religious belief but to our conditioning within those beliefs. Christians are committed to a belief that The Word is the creative and creating principle of the Godhead, The Mystery. We are also committed to a belief that "The Word was made flesh and dwelt among us." Such problems as we may experience stem, I suggest, from our natural tendency to shrink the big picture, to interpret everything in terms of Earth alone and our own Earth-experience.

In our encounters with persons, both similar and dissimilar to ourselves, who appear to be associated with the U.F.O. I suggest that we think it possible that we are encountering our own brethren. Whatever Mankind may be *in toto*, within the widest possible context, we may very well discover ourselves to be but one manifestation among a multitude in terms of the total Creature of whom we are persons.

It is at this point that our known and acknowledged flaws and failings take on a new significance. Our mythology enshrines the understanding that we are in some way alienated, in loss of our integrity and in a state of banishment, however that may be understood. The mythology may even be the articulation of deep collective memory in this respect. From this whole sense of dis-ease the whole apparatus of religion arises as an urgent attempt to mend fences, recover lost ground, restore communication and discover wholeness.

Whatever the differences between the great world religions, or indeed between the sophisticated and the primitive, these common threads run through all of them. They variously acknowledge dis-order and they variously point towards wholeness. In their different ways they all look beyond the frontiers of this life and their differing mythologies involve a Cosmic dimension which is the context of Earthly life and to which this Earthly life relates.

There is lodged within the folk-memory, the collective unconscious – call it what you will – an awareness of primaeval catastrophe which finds its expression in mythology all over the world. Legends, such as the "lost continent" of Atlantis, provoke years of search and speculation by a wide spectrum of interested parties, ranging from the serious scholar to the occultist. The banishment of Adam and Eve from Paradise is capable of all manner of interpretation in the hands of a skilful preacher but, I suggest, it may be no less capable of interpretation as reflecting the consequences of a dis-order in mankind which is not Earthly in origin at all, but Cosmic. The "Garden of Eden," however we may come to understand it, may never have been an Earthly set of circumstances in the first place.

Our situation, perceived by science – popularly at least – as one of being apparently alone in a vast, dead and apparently meaningless Universe, is capable of interpretation, theologically, in terms of a banishment. The challenge to our theological thinking, posed by the eruption into our consciousness of seemingly inexplicable visitants, is one of *raising our sights*. It is a challenge *to think bigger in Faith*, for it is only the Faith which will enable us to make sense of it at all.

SEEING OURSELVES?

Robert Burns, in one of his most memorable and delightful poems, gives us these thoughtful lines upon which to ponder:

> *O wad some Pow'r the giftie gie us*
> *To see oursels as others see us!*
> *It wad frae monie a blunder free us*
> *An' foolish notion.*

From the experiences of a multitude who have encountered persons who are seemingly Extra-Terrestrial, it is not too difficult to put ourselves in the place of our visitors and make the attempt to which Burns refers. Nor is it, I suggest, too foolish a notion to attempt to do so.

Here is a world, a planet, an environment – however our visitors perceive it – which is other than their own and to which they feel drawn in order to investigate, thus to understand. In addition – and I shall return to this on a later page – some at least feel the need to make personal contact with Earth-Aliens and enter into person-to-person relationships, as best they may, of a mutually respectful and beneficial nature.

What do they discover? A creature who is of the same order as themselves, but differently evolved. There is a puzzling identity with other sentient creatures of a lower order altogether – animals, in other words. Furthermore, like these animals, the Earth-Alien is not androgynous (as certain, at least, of our Extra-Terrestrial brethren seem to be) and is thus found in two closely related forms, both being necessary for the reproduction of the species.

Furthermore, and most oddly, the Earth-Alien is sustained, in terms of the renewal of his life-energies, by the consumption of both vegetation and – almost incredibly – *other animals* which are not, biologically, dissimilar to himself! (This, however extraordinary, being also an observed feature of animal life.) There is an identifiable life-cycle, shared with the animal order and – curiouser and curiouser! – the Earth-Alien, again like the animals, also requires the peculiar atmospheric circumstances of his environment in order to remain alive.

The Earth-Alien – our very own brother, no less – clearly abides in a most disturbing ambience of dis-equilibrium. His technology, therefore, is obliged to be crudely mechanical and of a truly bewildering complexity. His mind is too generally dis-equilibriated to be able, almost to conceive, let alone to participate in the mind/apparatus partnerships which are normal.

Our Earth-Alien brother is thus our brother indeed, but dissimilar in several respects, some of which are disturbing. Physically, he is a lumbering creature; half-us and half-animal. He shares the same mind as ourselves but there is much dis-order within it. His mind exhibits many positively self-destructive patterns and also appears to be, in some fields and at some levels, to be in a state best described as temporary shut-down. Nevertheless, there is that about him which attracts, and attracts exceedingly for, after all, he is our very own brother!

But what a business it is – and sometimes a hazardous one indeed – to enter our brother's environment! Moving on to the exact wavelength he inhabits is quite an alarming proposition. It is easier, and a lot less disturbing, to remain slightly off his wavelength but sufficiently close to it to establish contact. Thus, for the most part at least, we can see him, but – Alas! – he cannot see us.

The merit of such an admittedly speculative exercise as this is that it introduces the possibility that we, who are accustomed only ever to think of ourselves as the observer, might in fact be the observed. It further introduces the possibility that there are other ways than our own of being, and of physically, materially, expressing what I suggest is the common nature of the Creature, Mankind.

A DISTURBING POSSIBILITY?

There is yet another possibility which is introduced into our thinking processes and it is that our search for signs of organic life on other planets or their moons might, perhaps, be as pointless as it is plaintive. Life abounds; I suggest that the Universe is teeming with it, on wavelengths other than our own (the word "wavelength" being, probably, a metaphor in this application). Our religious mythology, if interpreted in terms of a somewhat bigger picture, might suddenly reveal to us the origins, and nature, of our apparent isolation on a "Devil's Island" set in a vast ocean of meaninglessness.

The observer and the observed tend to modify each other; this is a fact of scientific observation, certainly in the sub-atomic field of study. I suggest that our visitors may be modifying us and may themselves be in the process of modification by us. Our own increasing awareness of their visitations may indicate to us what we might, perhaps, interpret as the beginnings of the end of our isolation. In religious terms this is not too difficult to comprehend, even if our visitors – as *a symptom* of the end – are quite unexpected. Christian believers, of all people, ought to take phenomena of this sort – indeed of any sort – in their stride, for we are committed to belief in a *Parousia*, a consummation, a fulfilment of all things in Christ. The New Testament, at its very end, records the words of "the One sitting on the throne" saying:

> *"Now I am making the whole of creation new."*
> *(Rev 21: 5)*

Both observers and observed are involved in that process. I suggest that our visitors may be compelled now to rediscover their long-lost brethren by the stirrings of that very fundamental dynamic within them. It is also possible that, having no religion as we know it, they may lack certain insights which would enable them to understand why they have come, and are coming, from all points of the Cosmic compass.

CHAPTER FOUR

THE disciplines of science rightly concentrate upon the question, "what is it and how does it work?" They are applied as a result of encounters with phenomena, ranging from microbes to volcanos, and they involve specialist studies ranging from, let us say, geography to astrophysics. The disciplines of science are very properly rigorous and are maintained as objectively as the mortal human mind can be objective. Hypotheses are arrived at, and then they are tested until they either fail or prove themselves tenable.

Problems arise when the scientist strays beyond the competence of his discipline and announces, let us say, that there is no reality other than that which he is able to observe through his microscope. The most preposterous – almost endearing – example was voiced, not by a scientist but by a politician who claimed that, as a well-known Cosmonaut had been up into Space and had not seen God, there therefore was no God!

Problems also arise through the tightly compartmentalised thinking which can separate mechanics from meaning, expertise from guiding ethics. This, however, is a manifestation of the human condition and its inability to be "holistic" in practice, however "holistic" it may proclaim itself to be in principle.

Science may reasonably be expected to do one of two mutually contradictory things and, very probably, to do both at once. In respect of the U.F.O and its occupants, it will "hold the line" and maintain currently held and generally respected positions and hypotheses for as long as possible. The various disciplines – themselves compartmentalised and thus often incompletely in touch with each other – will apply their own present preferred positions until they are no longer tenable without modification. This is all entirely right and proper.

At the same time, and within the same disciplines, others will, tentatively at first, advance hypotheses as to "what" and "how" in response, either to a highly personal challenge, or to a nagging fascination with what the U.F.O. presents as *a challenge in reality*, and not as the figment of a disordered imagination.

Out of this usually painful but fundamentally creative tension, quantum leaps in human understanding have been made in times past, and in most – if not all – fields of scientific study. I suggest that we may confidently expect as much again with – alas! – the built-in paranoia of mortal, earthly humanity keeping one eye open for the possible military use of anything that might emerge therefrom.

THE THIRD DISCIPLINE

There is, however, another discipline, a field of study, which lies between science and religion and which tends to encroach upon the territory of both. It is a field of study almost universally misunderstood and very extensively mis-applied. It is a field of study which carries with it considerable dangers of Ego inflation and it is beset with all manner of hazards. It is, furthermore, a field of study which is almost impolite to mention in respectable religious or scientific company, and yet it has to do with the profoundest realities. It cannot be ignored in our present study, for it is essentially concerned with *the expansion of the field of consciousness* and the coming to terms with realities not normally perceived.

I refer, needless to say, to that field of study generally known as "the Esoteric" or "the Occult." Parts of it have been encroached upon already by science, in the disciplines of Parapsychology and Jungian Psychology, and are thus made respectable. But the word "occult" simply means "hidden" and generally refers to what we might conveniently describe as the psychic nuts and bolts of creation. It further has to do with what Jungians usefully describe as The Collective (or Universal) Unconscious.

The emotional reaction of a great many religionists to the word "occult" – however vigorously they themselves, all unwittingly, encroach upon it – tends to be immediately unfavourable. It has to be admitted (by a "religionist!") that this is usually a reaction based upon two things. The first is a profound ignorance mingled with a deep fear. The second – and the more seemly – arises from encounters with, and ministry to, individuals who have been damaged – sometimes badly – by blatant mis-application of the energies that can be released when things of an inner, psychic nature are irresponsibly tampered with.

The tendency therefore, particularly among those whose religious tradition is rationalistic and uneasy with the mystical, is to identify this whole field with "the devil and his angels." A more considered view would, I suggest, advocate a proper caution and restraint, not because the field of esoteric study is intrinsically "evil" but rather *because it is holy!* Respect, based upon an acknowledgement both of ignorance and of uncertain motivation, is more becoming in any event – let alone wiser – than an enthusiastic tinkering with the unknown, armed with a "knowledge" that is almost certain to be both fragmentary and specious.

Cleared of all subjective and emotional reactions to it, the occultist's field of study may best be understood as that of the inner structures beneath the outer, and of the energies involved therein. The aim of the white magician has already been stated, in another context. It is "to know in order to serve." Thus stated, it is admirable. Problems arise, however, as a result of the built-in weaknesses of the human condition, and of these the individual is seldom his own best judge. This point is important, for what we may describe as *the subject matter itself* is morally neutral – it just *is*. It is the student himself who is, always, the source and cause of such mischief as may ensue, for the temptations to manipulate, to use, to mis-apply and to inflate the Ego in the process are many and subtle. The distinction between "white magic" and "black magic" – and all the shades of grey between them – depends entirely upon the magician himself and his own inner motivation.

Occult study, properly understood and embarked upon, is a disciplined bringing into consciousness and understanding of *that which is already known*. Already known in that it is part of the human heritage of intuition, instinct, folk-memory and psychic awareness of which all men and women are partakers, and of which a great many are half-aware, instinctively half-knowing, sensitive in a multitude of different ways. Serious students of the occult are quick to describe it as a science, and this is not without some justification, though its methodologies, though claimed to be exact, are not those of the conventional laboratory.

MUDDY WATERS?

The study and understanding of the psychic nuts and bolts of creatures, and of man's earthly environment, is the aspect of occult study which might be seen as encroaching upon the field of conventional science. There is another aspect, however, inextricably interwoven with the first, which some might consider to be an encroachment upon the field of religion. It is the urgent concern of the serious, practising occultist to become "contacted upon the Inner Planes."

The establishment of contact with what are known as "inner plane adepti," learning from them and working with them, is a feature of serious, magical occultism. Within less overtly magical circles, numerous esoteric schools have emerged, dedicated to the collection and dissemination of the teachings of this, or that, discarnate luminary. At another level, but allied to both, is mediumistic activity of all kinds, manifesting the natural gifts and awarenesses of a great variety of individuals.

LOOKING IN THE WRONG DIRECTION

Having introduced the esoteric, or occult, field of concerns it is now necessary to emphasise that, whatever its merits or demerits may be, *it is essentially irrelevant in itself* to our current attempt to come to terms with the reality of the U.F.O. and its occupants. Why is this so?

Occultism – or, if you prefer, esotericism – is essentially concerned with the psychic nuts and bolts of the Earth-state, with understanding how things work at levels other than the everyday, and with the possibilities of management – responsible or irresponsible – of such energies as are discovered therein. In the process, it usually takes for granted *post-mortem* states of life and consciousness and trusts that they may be – at least in part – usefully concerned with the general Earthly well being. In consequence of this it seeks to bridge the gaps for the better management, by the presently incarnate, of their own earthly lives.

It must be recognised that the whole field of esoteric/occult concern is vast and exceedingly varied. It extends, for example, into all forms of alternative medicine and healing techniques for it is essentially concerned with the rediscovery of that, within the natural order, which is already known by mankind but has – especially within rationalistic cultures – become overlaid or forgotten.

I suggest that this whole field can only be usefully approached without those prejudgements which are based upon a mixture of misunderstanding, ignorance and fear. It is also better approached, I suggest, without too much enthusiasm! It will then be seen for what it is: an essentially Earth-bound field of interest and concerns, from first to last and from top to bottom. To say this is to pass no judgements, it is simply to be as accurate as it is possible for fallible mortals to be.

That there are hazards involved in certain practices is obvious, and is readily acknowledged by the responsible practitioner. That the usefulness, safety or danger of a great deal of this hangs – hazardously – upon personal motivation is also generally acknowledged. That misuse and mis-application for personal ends can – and does – take place is well known and deplored. That the necessary gifts of discernment are not always adequate to the task in hand is sometimes less readily acknowledged, and that the whole esoteric/occult field of interest lends itself, all too readily, to all the enthusiasms of a new and exciting counterfeit of religion is not always recognised either. Nevertheless, these are human failings and weaknesses. The subject-matter just *is*, and it – or parts of it – may, or may not, be the legitimate concerns of mortal, human men or women. This is not a judgement which it is our present concern to make, even if we were infallibly competent to make it!

Why, therefore, introduce into our discussion of the U.F.O, its crew, and their challenge to our religious and scientific world-views, a whole field of study and concern which is, in itself, essentially irrelevant to the discussion, quite apart from its ability to provoke negative emotional reactions from both scientist and religionist?

There are two answers to this question that I would suggest. The first is that *it is very necessary to establish its essential irrelevance.* The second is to bring into our awareness certain human faculties, and also certain types of proposition which, rightly understood and applied, will be of considerable assistance to us in coming to terms with a great deal of the human experience of the U.F.O. and its occupants. Of these, more later.

THE ESSENTIAL BLESSEDNESS OF NATURE

First of all, however, it will be useful to remind ourselves that everything so far dealt with is part of what we might conveniently describe as Nature. Within its own parameters, science is the investigation of nature. Within somewhat different parameters, the esotericist, the occultist, also investigates nature, but concentrating more upon what we might describe as its inner faces rather than the outer. All human faculties involved are entirely natural, integral parts of the common human nature in which certain faculties are variously emphasised in different individuals. It is important to be reminded by the first Chapter of the Book of Genesis that, in respect of everything that was created:

God saw that it was good

Of itself, Nature is wholly good. Certain aspects of the natural order are more vulnerable than others to manipulation, misuse or even perversion by dis-ordered minds. Disturbed from their proper places and natural equilibrium, some creations within the natural order can pose hazards to others, but this, I suggest, is commonly the product of dis-order in manipulating minds: scientific, occult and religious! It reflects not at all upon nature itself.

The Christian Revelation will have none of the Zoroastrian dualism which, in various intellectual guises, has infected the thinking of many Western Christians over the centuries. The Christian Revelation, as indeed the Hebrew tradition which lies behind it, entirely refutes any and every suggestion that "the material" is in some sense inferior, or even intrinsically evil, and only "the spiritual" is good, or holy. The Incarnation makes precious nonsense of all that!

Our subject, so far, has been Nature; natural creation, the natural order, human nature, the natural and very varied human faculties. Nature must emphatically include the U.F.O. and its occupants, just as it must also include the home-bases and home-environments that our various visitors temporarily leave behind them. Unimaginable they might seem to us to be – at the present moment – but part of the same Nature they undoubtedly are, for the whole of Nature abides within The Mystery and it is all, *of itself*, created good.

NATURE AND GRACE

The Christian Revelation, however, is the introduction of a wholly new "contract for existence," a wholly other set of opportunities for, as we have already been reminded:

"Now I am making the whole of creation new."

The Incarnation, the beginning of the New Creation, raises all the potential of Nature – and in the first instance, human nature – to a plane which is wholly other and which represents the perfection, fulfilment and transfiguration both of the natural order itself and, in the process, the human faculties. Nature is in process of fulfilment and transfiguration by the Divine Grace. It is, therefore, necessary to state, without reserve, the essentials of Christian belief and expectation, for only in this context can we hope to make sense of the experiences that provoke this current study.

Christian belief begins with The Incarnation and it is a faith, based upon experience both past and continuing, that:

"God in Christ was reconciling the world to himself." (2 Cor 5: 19)

Church doctrine must be understood as poetry rather than as prose, for the realities which it seeks to express are always greater than any possible modes of human expression. In the person of Jesus the Christ, the two natures, that of Divinity (the Creator) and that of Humanity (the creature) were, and are forever, united. The purpose of The Incarnation, and thus the mission of Christ, is the uniting of the creature, Mankind, with its Creator in a wholly new Creation. To this end;

"Christ died for our sins, in accordance with the scriptures." (1 Cor 15: 3)

"In accordance with the scriptures" means, in this context, in full character and congruity with the unfolding revelation of God, and of the human condition in relation to its Creator, that is found in the Hebrew Bible, known to Christians as The Old Testament.

The Incarnation simply means an entry into the earthly human condition and the free and loving acceptance of the inevitable consequence of that entry. Human paranoia, self-destruction and the perversions both of truth and of the law which sought to enshrine the truth, could do no other than combine to destroy the insupportable Presence. Naturally enough, given the prevailing circumstances of perverted nature, this was solemnly done in the name of Religion and Law.

Death was accepted and suffered as the inevitable consequence of entry into the perverted human condition. It was interpreted by the Sufferer, in advance of his suffering, as the fulfilment, once and for all, of all that the sacrificial apparatus of religion had, gropingly, sought to accomplish. Jesus was the one and eternal scapegoat. In his death, the human race died by its own hand. In his resurrection, the human race is re-created. How so? *Because there is but one Creature – Mankind – of which each individual is a person.* The one and the many are incapable of separation. In the poetry of an ancient credal statement, therefore, the Incarnation was effected –

... not by conversion of Godhead into flesh: but by taking manhood into God ... not by confusion of substance, but by unity of person.

The totality of the Creature is thus modified in principle. I suggest that it may very well be interpreted as a whole new contract for human existence.

The many and the one cannot be separated, for Mankind is a unity and thus Everyman and Everywoman experiences all, and only, the experience of Mankind, the total creature. What happens to one happens to all. The killer is also the killed, the torment within the individual is the torment at the heart of the whole. This manifests in projection from person to person of the self-destruction within and in what may be described as an institutionalised and mutual paranoia.

A DOCTRINE OF RE-CREATION

The Incarnation represents the re-creation of the total Creature, for what happens in one modifies the many because it goes straight to the heart of the whole. The Incarnation may thus be understood as *a process* as well as an historical event. It is the once-only-and-forever Mystery and, I suggest, it marks, in terms of Time, the beginning of what we might describe as The Cycle of Redemption. The fulfilment and completion of that Cycle is promised in that Mystery which we proclaim as The Second Coming, concerning the timing of which we are forbidden to speculate, and the scenario of which we are discouraged from trying to write!

In the meantime, mortal men and women who are Christian Believers are charged with the task of spreading the Good News to their brethren for the love of them and, above all, for Christ's love of them.

The process of re-creation is interior, not external. The work of the Divine Grace within the individual is to transfigure, and to raise the whole being and all its innate gifts and faculties, on to a wholly other plane. The individual Believer, therefore, has the duty to positively seek transfiguration, even in this mortal life, by the free gift of heart and will and by wholehearted cooperation with the Divine Grace working within. This is seldom effected without the profoundest of trauma but it is done, not for love of self but for love of God. It is undertaken, not for self but for others, for the whole Creature, Mankind, is transfigured in and through its persons and its persons are re-created from within the depths of the total Creature. The one lives for the many, that the total Creature may be deified.

This process does not stop with the Creature, Mankind, for in ways unimaginable and impenetrable, the whole Creation is to be made new. The transfiguration of the totality of what we know as the Natural Order is involved, therefore, and Mankind has a central part to play in this process.

This being the scope of the Vision, it follows that this is by no means a narrowly "religious" concern, but a Cosmic, all-embracing process of thought within the Mind of The Mystery. If the question should then arise: "What has this to do with all these little men in flying saucers?" the reply is: "Everything!" For, as St Paul puts it, the totality of things is in process of being *summed-up in Christ*. I suggest that what we are experiencing, in our encounters with our apparently Extra-Terrestrial brethren, is *a convergence*, for they too are involved, in their own ways and according to their own needs, in the deification of that very Creature, Mankind, of which they too are all persons.

CHAPTER FIVE

EVERYTHING that we have dealt with so far may be broadly categorised under the heading of "Nature." Science has to do, exclusively, with Nature. Occultism is concerned with Nature, in certain of its inner aspects. Religion is the child of disordered Nature and starts from Nature in order to reach, in its many and varied ways, towards a higher category. The entire Universe is Nature; the Universe, that is to say, that we see, observe and encounter. And our apparently Extra-Terrestrial visitors are also Nature, as are their currently unknown and unimagined homelands.

The Incarnation, however, modifies the totality of Nature. Nature is, we might say, modified in principle; the new potential is there to be realised and the New Creation is in process of formation, *from within*. The Divine Grace, at work in an individual who is open to it, and able both to receive and respond, transforms, transfigures, and finally *deifies*. We dare to use that last, awesome, word because the union of God and Mankind is the whole purpose of the Incarnation. This was no fence-mending exercise; it was a union of the two natures, Godhead and Manhood, in order that Earthly Man may not be merely restored to the place from which he had fallen, but rather re-created in union with his Creator. There is, I suggest, no putting back of clocks in Timelessness!

Words are hopelessly inadequate, and so profound is the Mystery that no language, even that of poetry or myth, can hope to do it justice. We dare not "water it down," however, for if we do, we deny Christ. All diminishments are denials; we must face the unimaginable head-on, for Jesus the Christ was not just a good man who said wise things; he was, and is, and shall be forever, The Incarnation. While respectful of the religious tradition into which he was born, he transcended it absolutely and, in effect, made the whole of Religion redundant. During the course of the Cycle of Redemption, which began, in Time, with the Nativity of Christ and will be fulfilled at the Second Coming, religion is working out its own redundancy. Only in that context, and in that clear understanding, can a "Christian Religion" make any sense at all.

CONCERNING HEAVEN

"Heaven" is variously understood, both by the great world religions and by individuals. In terms of the Christian Revelation it is to be understood as a state of being, a state of re-creation and, above all, as a participation in the New Relationship between Mankind and its Creator.

It is not possible either to define or to describe an intense personal relationship. An intense personal relationship, always and inevitably, partakes of the nature of mystery and is thus, by definition, incapable of definition! A love-affair has to be lived and experienced; its mystery can only be communicated to other lovers. The Biblical imagery of Bridegroom and Bride, emphasised and indeed fulfilled in the New Testament, provides us with the only language which is in any sense adequate as a means of articulation of the mystery.

The mystical saints testify to this, and the poetry of St John of the Cross, referring to the "inner darkness" of the process of re-creation puts it thus:

> *Oh noche, que juntaste*
> *Amado con amada*
> *Amada en el Amado transformada!*

Which the South African poet Roy Campbell, in his translation, renders:

> *Oh night that joined the lover*
> *To the beloved bride*
> *Transfiguring them each into the other.*

Heaven is the state of re-creation, and Heaven is also the state of having been re-created from within, and thus released both *to be, and to become*, on a wholly other plane of being altogether. Heaven is a state of conscious, loving relationship, and Heaven is to be understood as the truly human Community – the New Humanity – which shares a common mind which is the Mind of Christ.

The Citizen of Heaven is, in no way whatsoever, to be thought of as a "clone of Jesus!" Neither is Heaven to be cosily anticipated as simply a one-to-one of "me and Jesus!" Heaven is nothing if not corporate and Heaven is totally dynamic, for it represents a wholly new train of thought – *an entirely new Inner World* – within the Mind of The Mystery whom we call Almighty God.

THE IMAGE OF GOD

Mankind is made *in the image of God*; so the very first chapter of the Book of Genesis tells us. This "imagehood" is frequently interpreted in strictly moral terms; free-will, and the knowledge of right from wrong, are advanced as its essence. I suggest that this is a profoundly superficial interpretation and that two other faculties must have the prior claim.

The first is that of *Mind, and the creative imagination*. Every child has a universe of creatures swarming in his or her mind. The world of the imagination is the greatest of our human riches. There is neither difficulty nor discord in our happily flitting from one interior world to another, nor of "cross-fertilising" one with another; we all do it, all day long. There is no end to our creations and there is no end to the life of the creatures that swarm within the human mind. Both will, however, reflect the character of the mind that thinks them.

The second, related, facet of our "imagehood" is that of *creativity itself*. Mankind is created to be a co-creator with the Creator of all, as the second – and older – chapter of Genesis makes plain. However primitive, however simple the creations of men and women may be, they represent something fundamental to their very humanity. As soon as creativity ceases in an individual, so does life itself, and the greatest harm that can be inflicted on a child is the stifling, or inhibiting, of his or her imagination and creative instincts. Even wanton destructiveness is a form of misapplied creativity, often the fruit of frustration. There is – as every small boy knows – an innate satisfaction in the making of a really good mess!

The mind of Man being all but limitless in its scope, the creative imagination of the Eternal Mind is altogether beyond the capacity of our crabbed and conceited attempts to limit it! Worlds abound. Entire Universes, quite other than our own, swarm within completely different "outer spaces" and in myriad dimensions, every one. There is not the slightest likelihood of the mortal, Earth-bound mind comprehending more than the most miniscule fragment of its own environmental experience. Better by far to let all go, to set and dance to the Lord of the

Dance, than to turn intellectually inward, in specious brilliance, and be as good as dead and buried in the coffin of one's own paltry brainbox!

TRANSFIGURATION AND ABSORPTION

In the essentially impossible task of trying to form a picture of the total scheme of things, it is perhaps as helpful an image-making as any to attempt to see the whole of the Natural Order being interpenetrated by, and in the process of absorption by, the Heavenly. Having attempted the formation of such an image, we must speedily dismantle it, lest it take unto itself all the limiting and distorting characteristics of an idol. Nevertheless it is true enough to mortal, Earthly man's experience. The work of the Divine Grace within individuals – and thus within societies and institutions – is a matter of experience and, in the context of the life of prayer, both the distinction between the Heavenly and the Earthly, and also the process of transformation by the latter into the former, is both known and lived. It is, however, impossible of any coherent and narrowly rational articulation.

It need not surprise us, therefore, to find Heaven both deeply involved in – *although wholly other than* – the apparent convergence of hitherto separated parts of the Natural Order. Whatever awareness our Extra-Terrestrial visitors may have of the Heavenly dimension is presently unknown to us. In any event it is likely to be different from our own. It may be the case that Earthly Man, being the most disordered and dysfunctional part of the Total Creature, is – potentially at least – the most closely aware of the Heavenly dimension. The Incarnation was, and is, a work of redemption and re-creation. Beyond doubt both we on Earth and our Extra-Terrestrial brethren have an infinity to learn from each other and – who knows – an Eternity in which to learn it?

The great bulk of the published accounts of the encounters of mortal men and women with Extra-Terrestrials, visually perceived and physically experienced, give the impression of somewhat intrusive visitants, though essentially benign and anxious not to do actual harm. I suggest that the more normal approach of the Extra-Terrestrial shows a greater maturity and sensitivity. It is characterised by a respectful diffidence, a concern to avoid being the cause of alarm, and it appears quick to recognise an essential identity and thus, equality. Acceptance is sought, even friendship.

To be treated, by the more brash, and arguably less mature, "species" of Extra-Terrestrial as a zoological specimen is rather beneath our own concept of human dignity. It is, however, a salutary reminder of the ways in which Earthly Man approaches his animal brethren, all too often with scant regard for *their* dignity. Perhaps it becomes us ill to be excessively affronted by the enthusiasms of the less mature among our visitors!

PROVISIONAL CONCLUSIONS

The suggestion is here made that our experiences of the Extra-Terrestrial are essentially objective and real; that there is a common, underlying dynamic which is prompting an increasing – and increasingly varied – pattern of visitations. I suggest that this may very well represent a process of convergence, or coming-together, of that which has been long separated and that the apparent isolation of Earthly Man on one planet of a seemingly "dead" Universe may be in the process of coming to its end.

I suggest that all this is essentially consistent with the New Testament hope and expectation of the *Parousia*, but that it is, as yet, only symptomatic of it. I suggest that this whole pattern of experience has to do with that process of transfiguration and absorption of the Natural Order into the Heavenly and wholly other. And I suggest that The Incarnation, into the most damaged and dysfunctional of all the species of the Total Creature, Mankind, is not just for the sake and salvation of Earthly Man alone, but for the transfiguration of all. There may very well be, for Earthly Man, a measure of *priesthood* involved, however this may be understood, but of this – as of much else – we are currently obliged to wait and see.

PART TWO ⊙

Making Sense of the Impossible.
A Necessary Riot of Speculations

PROLOGUE TO PART TWO

Where's the philosopher who can relate,
with simple and surpassing clarity,
what is – in the Eternal Charity –
the E. T. Alien's own post-mortem state?

Say: does it haunt their every mortal breath –
always supposing that they breathe at all,
are not sustained by Energies, withall
beyond our ken – this daily fear of death?

Do they re-cycle through some aeons other,
refining their technologies the while
to ever new perfection? In what style
am I related to my "other" brother?

And in their worlds do boatmen cross the Styx
with Alien wraiths, borne out of sight and mind
to "underplanets" of a different kind?
And what reaction to a Crucifix?

Or are we, as I fancy, brothers all,
with Earthmen paranoid, projecting fear;
more terrified the closer they draw near
who are untouched by Adam and his fall?

Does Heaven orchestrate Heaven's own desire
as persons of one creature – wavelengths other
but fast merging – recognise a brother?
To all-transcending Heaven do all aspire?

We have arrived at a position wherein our Extra-Terrestrial brethren are taken seriously as real people who really exist. We are now obliged to enter a realm which is anathema both to religious and scientific academia. It is the realm of speculation.

Speculation is only a danger to truth, however, when it masquerades as something other than it is and, in the context of such a masquerade, both religious and scientific academia are entirely right to recoil from it. But speculation, as a means of arriving at possible hypotheses for later rigorous testing, is an entirely proper exercise and cannot be dispensed with. We are bound, therefore, to make a distinction between what we actually *know* (according to currently accepted criteria of knowledge) and that concerning which we can only *speculate*.

Speculation is fuelled and informed by the intuitive faculty but until it is thoroughly interrogated by the reason, it retains the status of guesswork, more or less inspired. The proof of the speculative pudding is always in the eating. We may speculate to our hearts' content but the *status* of our speculations must always remain quite clear.

For my own part, I have had cause to become satisfied as to the objective reality of my Extra-Terrestrial brethren. That is my private judgement in the matter. Over a period of years, and in a number of different ways, I am left with no reasonable doubts. The sceptical reader (if any such remain with me) must therefore interpret what follows as the first stumbling attempts of such a one as myself to make sense – by openly acknowledged speculation – of what has begun to suggest itself as a result, not of any kind of "abduction" experience, but of *repeated encounters with persons* which have issued in a sense of mutual, brotherly affection and respect.

CHAPTER SIX

I AM encouraged to believe that there is, not one group of Extra-Terrestrials currently engaged in the exploration of ourselves and our environment, but several very different groups – even a great many. I suggest that we may begin to discover among them a well-nigh astonishing diversity, both in appearance and in mode of development, but all within the single creature, mankind. We are, I insist, confronted with beings who are *essentially human* and, apart from such accidents as appearance, essentially the same human beings as ourselves.

HUMAN AND HUMANOID

Here I must introduce a caveat, for I am encouraged to believe that the more intrusive, and occasionally visible, of our visitors may not be fully human but rather *humanoid*, operating under the direction of human Extra-Terrestrials and performing tasks on their behalf. It is as if we, on Earth, were able to genetically engineer a chimpanzee who was capable of operating equipment, and even carrying out simple surgical procedures, under a human direction which was at some remove. This, although somewhat fantastic a notion, is by no means as far-fetched as it would have seemed a generation ago. I suggest that most, if not all, the "abductions" and more intrusive visitations – not to mention physical examinations – that an increasing number of individuals claim to have experienced, are carried out by humanoids under remote human direction. The humanoids themselves are not machines, however. They are subordinates who may well have their own views regarding the things they are called upon to do.

I suggest that there may be more than one mode of investigation and exploration of our environment by remote-control. I am encouraged to think that mind/machine technology (for want of a better expression) is further advanced than anything in our current experience. I shall return to this subject on a later page.

I suggest that the great mass of visitants to us and to our environment remain, for the most part, on what I can best describe as another wavelength, recognising that the word "wavelength" may be but a metaphor for something similar but outside our current experience and usual understanding of things. If this is the case, being just "off-wavelength," they are both at less hazard from the unfamiliar dangers of our environment and are also able to observe us without – in the main – being themselves observed by the Earthly human eye or detected by our radar early warning systems.

WHERE DO THEY COME FROM?

The thorny question, "from where do they come?" must now be addressed and we are faced, immediately, with a sense of the utmost unreality, for the answers that might have sprung to the minds of a former generation will not serve us now. Our current knowledge of other planets of the Solar System is such as to discourage any notion that sophisticated civilisations are to be found there. Indeed their apparent natures are such as to preclude any realistic possibility of life, as we know it, being supported on any of them.

In respect of the rest of the stars and their planetary bodies in our own Galaxy we are, for all intents and purposes, completely in the dark. Distances are measurable in light-years and millions of light-years. We are left, I suggest, with two possible alternatives, both in the highest degree speculative.

The first is that our visitors may all be inhabitants of our own planet Earth, but as it exists upon other "wavelengths" than our own. (Remember the probable metaphoric nature of that word "wavelength.") Our brethren may thus be "wavelength-hopping" while remaining essentially "at home." The whole of Extra-Terrestrial phenomena may not, therefore, be Extra-Terrestrial at all but rather *Other-Wavelength-Terrestrial* and thus an essentially Earthbound business.

If this is the case, then investigations of an essentially psychic, or occult, nature might suggest themselves, for psychism and the occult are profoundly, and essentially, Earthbound in their concerns, seeking already to probe other post-mortem and Inner-Plane "wavelengths" of Earth-existence.

Certain it is that manifestations of the intuitive faculty, employed in psychic and occult activity, play a part in a great many of our encounters with our Extra-Terrestrial brethren. But the gifts of clairvoyance, clairaudience and clairsentience are normal, natural human faculties, variously bestowed but somewhat obscured in our own day by the overlays of sophisticated and rationalistic society. They are also – and entirely mistakenly – feared as potentially demonic by certain of the more rationalistic kinds of religionist. The same is true of thought-transference, or telepathy, which is also a feature of certain of our encounters with the Extra-Terrestrial.

These gifts referred to belong to human nature and, transformed by the Divine Grace, enter the truly spiritual realm in the mystical degrees of prayer. They are not, therefore, to be feared or identified with darkness; they are God-given and to be treated with the appropriate respect.

That our Earth lives its lives on many levels and on a multiplicity of "wavelengths" I am personally left in no doubt, but I find myself encouraged to believe that our Extra-Terrestrial brethren are not simply alternative-Earthly-wavelength brethren who are suddenly enabled to be nosey neighbours and are thus to be found peering across the garden fence. I suggest that, despite our difficulties of comprehension or imagination, they are Extra-Terrestrials indeed.

A PREFERRED ALTERNATIVE

The second alternative concerning the home base, or bases, of our visitors involves an extension of the first suggestion. For if this planet, Earth, exists and lives upon a multitude of levels and – to use our metaphor – "wavelengths," it is most unlikely that this is other than the case with the entire Universe – or indeed Universes, for why must there be but one?

It follows at once that, should this be the case, what we know as the observable Universe is only what we are able to observe of it from the standpoint of our own "wavelength" on Earth, in the context of the mortal life-state. Not for one moment can we imagine it to look differently than it presently appears to us, or to be other than it seems to us to be, or indeed to behave differently than our observations and our mathematical calculations lead us suppose that it does.

Our difficulties lie partly in a determination to conceptualise everything on our own terms and in accordance with our own experience, and partly in that arrogance which is born of fear and which rejects out of hand anything that cannot be controlled by a governed mind and a flawed will. Just as the internal combustion engine (and other sorts of engine) can be governed, or de-rated, so as to inhibit its operation beyond a particular degree of possibility, so can the Earthly, mortal human mind be *governed and de-rated*. I suggest that this is a consequence of that human condition which Religion variously describes as The Fall and Original Sin, and which the Western Mystery Tradition of occultism equally religiously describes as The Prime Deviation.

Within our speculative framework of possibilities the second alternative is, I suggest, the more appealing. In any event we are faced with that which transcends all our own categories and conventional frameworks. It is better to be bold than timid, for nothing can be proven, one way or the other, at the time of writing.

COMPLICATING THE UNIVERSE?

Let us assume, therefore, that our visitors come from elsewhere than our own planetary environment on any of its possible dimensions or wavelengths, but from an *elsewhere* that is *other* in terms of the plane, dimension or wavelength upon which it exists. There would appear to be, however, a number of quite different groups of Extra-Terrestrial human beings (one at least of which appears to employ non-human humanoids to perform tasks on its behalf), and so we are faced with the possibility of an entire other-dimensional Solar System, even an other-dimensional Galaxy, parts at least of which provide a variety of home bases from which a very differing and *perhaps even differently evolved* collection of travelling visitors come.

I suggest that it may be easier for us to turn the problems that are here posed upon their heads and to think it possible that it is we ourselves – Earthly humanity – that is *other*. I suggest that it is the wavelength (or what you will) upon which we ourselves abide that is out of step and separated from that which represents normality. This is, perhaps, where scientific speculation and religious speculation are obliged to look to one another for help, for it is no great matter to extend our interpretation of the mythology of The Fall and to see, in Adam's expulsion from Eden, an Earthly humanity's expulsion from the rest of a human race which had not fallen in the same way. We ourselves, I venture to suggest, may be the odd man out!

If this is the case, then the dynamic which drives our many and disparate visiting brethren relates to a general desire to re-discover that which has been long-lost and which – for whatever reason and by whatever means – has begun to re-emerge on the just-discernible fringe of things. We, who are apparently alone in a dead and meaningless Universe, begin to resemble jail-birds on a cosmic Devil's Island. The Universe is only dead and meaningless from the standpoint from which we are able to observe and experience it.

COME BACK, GALILEO, ALL IS FORGIVEN!

We are now faced with difficulties akin to those which faced our forefathers when they were confronted with the inescapable, and for them unpalatable, fact that the Earth is not the centre of the Universe but part of a planetary system, in orbit with other planetary bodies round one star of an unimaginable multitude of stars. All this is now a commonplace but it is no easy matter for us to think it possible that our entire scientific vision and understanding of the Universe, while perhaps beyond reproach in itself, may be at the deepest of levels irrelevant to the total human case. It is easier by far to see ourselves as the only ones in step than to think it possible that we may be the only ones, in a multitude unimaginable, who are actually *out of step!*

Our difficulties in coming to terms with the Extra-Terrestrial visitor lie in the necessity of committing the hitherto unpardonable sins of thinking science religiously, and thinking religion scientifically. These difficulties are compounded by the engagement, from time to time, of some of those facets of the intuitive faculty which tend to be ill-regarded by both science and religion, Reformed religion in particular.

If we are, or have been, in a condition of estrangement or separation, the mechanics of which cause us scientific perplexities, we are bound to enquire if such an understanding is explicable, or even tenable, in religious terms.

THE INSIGHTS OF RELIGION

The mythologies of the world are full of references to an evil principle, which is other than human, but with which humanity is, to some degree at least, identified. The myth of Adam and Eve advances the Serpent as a primary source of temptation. Eve chose the Serpent rather than her own Creator. She then corrupted Adam in the same manner and they were both expelled from Paradise and made to work for their living. *They fell to a lower order of being as a consequence.*

The same essential message, in many different mythological forms, is to be met with in almost every culture. Fear is found to be a controlling emotion among mortal men and women. As mankind grew in sophistication the developed religions of the world sought to come to terms with the experienced mystery of objective evil, the evil and corrupting principle which is other than human but manifests typically, and most powerfully, in and through human beings and their institutions. A characteristic feature of all this is fear which tends to overpower obligations of love and mutual respect.

Zoroastrian dualism, and its various successors, proclaimed belief in two "gods," a good one and an evil one, in perpetual cosmic conflict. The emergence of this developed religious belief is a testimony to the depths of human experience of the evil principle. The challenge to mankind was to choose between them and assist in the struggle thereby. In its later, sophisticated forms as found in the various dualistic cults of the Mediterranean world, material creation, propagation and all things "earthly" were considered evil. Only the spiritual was understood to be good. Although dualism of this nature is an absolute contradiction of the Christian belief in the Incarnation, and indeed of the whole Biblical tradition, it has left its mark, in the Christian West, in a tendency towards world-rejection which is not only contradictory but arguably pathological.

The Biblical tradition faces the mystery of objective evil with the understanding of a created consciousness, of a prior and higher order than the human, as being the evil principle behind mankind's own corruption. The new Testament speaks, in poetic terms, of "war in Heaven" and of "the dragon and his angels" being cast out; cast down to the Earth, indeed, prior to their final judgement. The implication is that earthly mankind is caught up in a problem altogether bigger and at a profounder level than itself, but has become culpably tainted, corrupted and identified in some way with that which is being acted out on a bigger stage.

It is not really possible to say very much more than this, other than to note that the Incarnate Son of God took it exceedingly seriously, personalised the evil principle in its traditional name and called it poetically but unmistakable, "the prince of this world" who was to be "cast out," and mankind thus rescued from identification with it.

Poetry and myth represent the only ways in which an understanding of that which lies just beyond the frontiers of comprehension may be articulated and communicated. They articulate *that which is experienced*, and the experience of mankind, worldwide, has been of alienation from that which is fully Real; a sense of separation, exile and of bondage to fear. Beneath all that is experienced as good, positive and beautiful – and quite apart from the natural negatives that are bound to balance the positives, both in the individual's emerging personality and in everything else – there has lurked an alienating, self-destructive principle. It is experienced as both other than human and at the same time tending to attach to the negative aspects of the human personality until they turn pathological, self-destructive and even outright demonic.

A mythology which is neither religious in the normal sense, nor scientific, but which belongs rather to the world of occultism, speaks of this same alienation and separation in the supposed fates of Atlantis and Lemuria. There is, in all mythology, an element of long-buried folk-memory. Folk-memory, however, of what? And at what level? And on what plane of possible being? We don't know the answers and we do well to bear our ignorance in mind.

More than this need not now be said. Suffice it that Earthly, human experience and the almost world-wide interpretation of that experience, has been of bondage, alienation and separation from that from which it is disastrous – even tragic in the proper sense of that word – to be so separated. It is precisely this universal human experience which has brought Religion into being. *Religion is Earthly mankind's increasingly urgent attempt to discover what is wrong and put it right.* Religious insights are therefore full of support for a theory of possible estrangement of ourselves from our Extra-Terrestrial brethren as a by-product of a primary estrangement, rather than an estrangement, for whatever cause, of them from us!

CHAPTER SEVEN

It has now become necessary for us to speculate, not so much upon the frontier between the disciplines of science and religion, as upon that far more shadowed frontier between science and the occult. What we look for, from the occult side of that frontier, is *a terminology* and *a framework of ideas*. What this whole enquiry is obliging us to do is to empty out the contents of our watertight boxes, labelled "Religion," "Science," "The Occult," and all the rest, on to the floor and search the muddled heap for anything that will fit or serve. Our real difficulties in this seemingly disordered, exercise come less from the problems themselves than from the almost pathological watertightness of our various mental boxes. We make difficulties for our own selves.

ATMOSPHERE, OR AURA?

I now suggest that our Extra-Terrestrial visitor, from wherever he (or she) comes, is faced with the hazards of entry, not into the Earth's atmosphere – which may well prove to be irrelevant to our present study – but rather into *the Earth's Aura*.

The Aura is not easily defined. It is a pattern of force-fields, energy-fields and so forth, reflecting as much – if not more – of *the character* as of the energies of the creature whose aura it is. This is as true, I suggest, of planet Earth as it is of every human being. There are theories of the "subtle bodies" which are to be met with in occult studies, but they need not detain us now.

Our visitor, whatever the means of travel, is obliged to enter into an Aura and to feel the influences both of its energy-patterns and also of its essential character. I suggest that such an entry can be disturbing both to the Aura so entered, and even more to the one entering. Until acclimatised, or at least familiarised with the problems encountered, it can be a disturbingly – even dangerously – dis-equilibriating experience, for there is that about the Aura of planet Earth which is both *other* and disturbing in a manner quite foreign to our visitors. This – by way of parenthesis – may be the reason why certain of our visitors prefer to risk humanoid subordinates rather than themselves! Lest we react too unfavourably to such a notion, we do well to remember that we, ourselves, sent dogs and monkeys up in space-rockets before ever a man was put to such a hazard. We all then waxed mightily sentimental about the poor animals – after they were dead!

The hazards attendant upon entry into the Earth's Aura relate to a mode of operation as yet unknown by Earthly man and women but not altogether beyond their possibilities of imagination. Suffice it that the first requirement is *a complete equilibrium and unity of mind and purpose* among those involved in such an entry. Anything which dis-equilibriates one member of the group threatens all, for control of the operation is lost and the endeavour is paralysed until harmony is restored. There is that about the Earth's Aura which is dis-equilibriating to a high degree. This relates not to basic energy-patterns but to *character*.

From this state of affairs, which I suggest to be the case, it is possible to conclude that a characteristic of all those involved in that kind of travel which makes visits to Earth possible is a disciplined and profound mutual cooperation in action. There is a unity of mind, a collective harmony, which suggests a background which emphasises cooperation rather than competition. This contrasts starkly with the usual Earthly emphasis which is the other way round. There is, I suggest, no place for the freelance individualist in a mode of operation which involves total, collective unity of mental concentration. That such a *modus operandi* is possible at all demands a cultural background which makes it possible. This immediately distances our Extra-Terrestrial brethren from ourselves, among whom competition, from the very earliest age, is exalted almost to the status of a religious duty.

CONCERNING THE EARTH'S AURA

The Earth's Aura reflects the character of that with which it is identified. It must be a matter of speculation as to why Extra-Terrestrial visitation seems to be a comparatively recent phenomenon, so much so as to cause the sceptical to regard alleged sightings and encounters as symptoms of a mass hysteria. (There is also, needless to say, the distinct possibility of an hysteria of scepticism!) Speculation might find one answer to the problem in the possibility of recent advances in Extra-Terrestrial technology which have only now begun to make visitations possible. I suggest that such a view may reflect a measure of projection of our own recent history and circumstances upon our brethren.

Another speculative answer to the problem might maintain that visitation has always been going on but we have only recently begun to notice it, and take account of it in a comprehending way, our own technological advances having pushed forward the frontiers of our imagination.

Yet another view might be that visitation has always been a normal feature of terrestrial life, but has been interrupted for a period of time. Ancient cave-paintings and pictures of "gods" sitting on rocket-like contrivances in various parts of the world, combined with seemingly inexplicable and very ancient landscape sculptures, visible only from the air, might be said to encourage such a view.

A fourth speculative suggestion is that there may have been that about the Earth's Aura which, for an unknown period, rendered it impenetrable – perhaps even invisible – and which is only now "thinning out" sufficiently to make visitation possible, if still not without some hazard. Within the context of what must be complete speculation, I incline towards this latter view.

WHY DO THEY COME AT ALL?

We are bound to return, time and again, to the question – why do our visitors come at all? To this question only one answer would seem to satisfy. They are sent! They are sent, I suggest, on two levels of motivation. The first is by command of whatever hierarchical structure prevails in the various homelands from which they come. The second is the deep, underlying dynamic which transcends all and moves all. Whatever the consciousness of individuals might contain, they are coming *in order to welcome us back*.

Earthly human conceptions of space-travel have about them that which is but an extension of a former generation's obsession with colonial exploitation. Colonisation of other heavenly bodies and the mining of their resources are subjects that figure large in space exploration speculations. Our underlying motivations and inspirations – at a deeper level than these superficial obsessions – relate to those of our Extra-Terrestrial brethren but they are overlaid with all the contradictions and confusions of the Earthly human condition.

Perhaps the most morbid manifestation of all is the projection into a fictionalised "outer space" of the "cops and robbers," and "cowboys and indians" confrontations which issue in the taking for granted, by succeeding generations, that there must therefore be such catastrophes as "space-wars." I suggest that we have yet to discover to what extent this is a morbid projection of Earthly human paranoia and self-destruction. It is both an echo of, and a manifestation of the objective evil with which Earthly humanity has long been identified and from which it is now released. Release – the work of The Incarnation – is both *a Principle and a Process.* The Principle is forever established; the Process is ongoing. I suggest that this may relate both to the ability of our visitors to penetrate a hitherto impenetrable Earthly Aura, and also to the continuing hazards attending such visitations.

Travel presupposes not only a destination but also a place from which the journey began, the place where the decision to set out was made and whose circumstances made it possible. Of the home bases of our various visitors we have no knowledge whatever. It is already clear that there is a high probability that they exist upon another "wavelength" than our own. It is indeed upon another "wavelength" – in our perceptions – that the profoundest encounters with our Extra-Terrestrial brethren take place.

Mention has already been made of those gifts of the intuitive faculty which come into play in interior perceptions and encounters. On a purely natural level they operate on the essentially Earthbound levels commonly known as the *psychic.* Transformed by the work of the Divine Grace within the total personality, these same gifts operate on a wholly other level which can properly be called *spiritual.* They are sometimes brought into play in the context of mystical prayer. It is a fact of experience that these same gifts are also brought into play in the context of encounters with Extra-Terrestrial brethren. This would seem to suggest a kind of "third level" of operation but – I suggest – purely natural though such encounters are (i.e: neither psychic in the Earthbound sense, nor spiritual in the mystical sense), it is typically that intuitive faculty which is matured, aided, transformed by the Divine Grace which is best able to perceive, to discern and then *to relate without fear.*

A RECAPITULATION

It is time to recapitulate. This is an exercise which will have to be repeated several times during the course of this study. We may approach it thus:

1) The Unidentified Flying Object and its Extra-Terrestrial crew are objective realities. They are not the product of mass hallucination.

2) They come, not from another dimension, plane or "wavelength" of this planet Earth, but from elsewhere in the Cosmos.

3) They give the impression of an ability to "change wavelengths" – using that term in the clear understanding that it may be a metaphor for something similar but as yet unknown to us.

4) They come from, and return to, home-bases which are not readily imaginable by us in terms of the perceptions and understandings of Earthly humanity and may, therefore, exist upon another "wavelength," or "wavelengths," than our own altogether.

5) Our Extra-Terrestrial visitors are essentially *human*. That is to say that they are of the same Creature, Mankind, as ourselves but are differently – and variously – evolved in terms of their own environments.

6) There is a considerable number, and variety, of different visitors, coming from very different places. One group at least employs humanoid subordinates to perform what are often quite sophisticated tasks. These are, probably, the ones most often encountered visually and are, probably, the ones most usually involved in alleged "abductions" of Earthly men, women and children. There is neither malice nor malign intent in any of our Extra-Terrestrial visitors. They are not to be perceived as a threat to us in any way.

7) There is, in religious terms, considerable support for an understanding which would see these visitations as voyages of re-discovery, and that is we ourselves who are isolated and "out of step."

8) The understanding that these visitations, together with our own, essentially crude, space exploration programmes (and also our fictional fantasies in this respect), are manifestations of the same underlying dynamic in Creation, all relating to a central and transcending Purpose, is made tenable by several religious insights.

9) The possibility that planet Earth may manifest an Aura which has long proved impenetrable to Extra-Terrestrial visitation, is tenable in religious terms; as is the possibility that its impenetrability may be in process of dispersal.

10) The possibility that Earthly mankind's environment, apparently on a different "wavelength" to the rest, and our dependency upon crude Earthbound energy sources and means of life-support, may constitute a form of exile from the rest of a quite differently-circumstanced humanity, is tenable in the light of religious insights.

Encounter with Extra-Terrestrials poses a challenge, both to conditioned thinking in respect of life's fundamental questions *How* and *Why*, and to the integrity of the one so confronted. There are but two choices; to run away from the challenge and hide behind negatives and denials, or to face up to the challenge and make the very best of it that is possible. Speculation concerning experiences and encounters, and attempts to find a comprehensible framework of reference, eventually lead to a number of working hypotheses. All working hypotheses must then be subjected to honestly conducted testing, rigorously and perpetually. They must be, honestly and firmly, modified when found wanting.

The conditioned mind, fragmented and compartmentalised into a water-tight (and all too often, light-tight) box for every category of thought, is hard put to it to arrive at anything that will serve as a starting-point, and it is starting points only that we are here concerned with. The finishing point – should it be possible for any such thing to exist in a dynamic Creation – is in any case in a *wholly other* state of being altogether.

CHAPTER EIGHT

Our Extra-Terrestrial brethren are of many different races. Their places of origin have determined the development of each race and their appearances differ accordingly. Some are androgynous, others are manifest in both male and female persons. Some are closer to their Earth-brethren than others, both in general appearance and evolutionary experience. None, however, are likely to have been identified, in the way Earthly humanity has been, with an obviously evil, perverse or malicious principle which is external to themselves. Paranoia and a tendency towards both personal and corporate self-destruction are thus unlikely to be features of their lives or evolution.

TRIAL AND ERROR: EXTRA-TERRESTRIAL EVOLUTION?
All creatures evolve by a system of trial and error. All creatures are given the freedom both to *be* and to *become*. Their circumstances, their environments and the level of conscious potential bestowed at their creation, will lead them into a multitude of trials and errors, collisions, adaptations and manoeuvrings. Honest error has no moral connotation, it is a part of the process of *becoming*.

There is, therefore, a principle of *time* or *duration* throughout a Creation which nevertheless abides in the *timelessness* of an eternal present moment. There are time-space parameters which determine the life of every creature for, without such a framework, nothing could come into expression, manifestation, creation (the words, each with a different nuance, are inadequate but we can do no better), but it must be kept in the back of the mind, by some means or other, that space-time is *never* an Absolute.

I suggest that our brethren have evolved by trial and error. There is, in any human society, a tension between the *One* and the *Many*, the individual and society as a whole. Human beings are, every one, unique and distinct persons and never what we imagine clones to be. The *many* is the entire context of the *one*, but it is the sum of all the *ones* that constitutes the *many*. It must be expected, therefore, that our various brethren, in the differing contexts of their own evolution, will have managed the resolution of this fundamental tension differently.

Evolution, growth, realisation of potential, all this is a process which takes place both in the *One* and in the *Many*. In terms of the individual this presupposes – in that purely Natural order which we are now considering – a process of birth, growth and learning by trial, error and death, followed by birth again to continue the process. The essence of each individual, the archetypal "set of proportions" as someone once put it, resides ever in the heart of that Ultimate Mystery we call God. As our Extra-Terrestrial brethren belong to the purely Natural order in Creation, it is not difficult to put forward, as one working hypothesis, an evolutionary process at work within them which involves birth, death and re-birth.

Parallels with Earthly pre-Christian religious beliefs suggest themselves at once, but we must beware! Our Extra-Terrestrial brother *may not have a religion* such as we understand it. Religion, on Earth, is the product of alienation, a response to fundamental dis-integration within the individual and separation from that individual's true or archetypal self. This is experienced as at least a partial distancing from the Source of all Being which is God. This dis-integration in the One is then manifested in the Many, the underlying Principle of dis-integration being at work in both.

A second working hypothesis, based upon the conviction that our Extra-Terrestrial brethren are human, like ourselves, but somewhat differently evolved, concerns their various cultures which are capable of sending explorers on voyages of space-travelling discovery. This, I suggest, requires a background in which the One is subservient to the Many, and in which unity of mind and purpose are regarded as paramount.

The re-birth beliefs of most of pre-Christian religion on Earth suggest to us, as a working hypothesis, a pattern of Extra-Terrestrial human evolution, in the Natural order, uncomplicated by identification with a Principle of disorder. The Biblical tradition, however, may suggest patterns within an Extra-Terrestrial social order in which Law, and absolute conformity with what Law is perceived to be, are the guiding principles of such societies. Single-mindedness, common purpose and the validation of the individual only in terms of conformity and observance will produce, in any society not dis-equilibriated and dis-integrated by the influence of objective evil, a steadily evolving evolutionary pattern which will realise all the potential within the Natural order to the full. It may indeed be the case that some, at least, of our Extra-Terrestrial brethren are already close to the limits of their potential.

I suggest that the individual can contribute to the totality only in an essentially – even completely – non-individualistic way. I suggest that anything that approaches maverick individualism is discouraged – even forbidden – as a threat to Society as a whole. Parallels to this may be found in primitive societies on Earth. The Law, as it is understood, is paramount and forgiveness for breaches of it may be unthinkable because never previously thought. The very principle of forgiveness may seem positively threatening on first encounter. It is, after all, regarded as immoral in a number of non-Christian religious systems on Earth!

SPECULATION, AND MORE SPECULATION!

All of this is speculation. All of it is, at best, a working hypothesis constructed, if not completely in advance of events, then substantially in advance of them. Time alone will prove or disprove this, that or the other detail. Our Extra-Terrestrial brethren come and go; they actually impinge upon the lives and consciousness of a few, however much the popular *idea* of them may fascinate the many.

Officialdom is full of denials, but denials are transparent because the workings of the official mind, and the political mind, are now very well known to the many and thus they are equally transparent. What officialdom *really* knows, however, it will kill to conceal. The corrupt and the manipulative will seek, by every means, to corrupt and to manipulate for advantage, but these are symptoms of an Earthly human condition which, I suggest, is not shared by our Extra-Terrestrial brethren, however many errors they may have made in their trials. They come, almost entirely, to look, to meet, to greet and to befriend. Whatever the reaction of the individual might be, upon encounter with his hitherto unsuspected brethren, the reaction of officialdom is to issue denials with one hand and scramble interceptors with the other; to compromise the career prospects of the honest witness who does not keep silent and to hope – by whatever means – to steal a technological march on potential Earthly rivals and enemies. Such is our very own human condition here on Earth.

The contrast between the Extra-Terrestrial visitor, as perceived and as experienced by some, and our own Earthly condition is stark indeed. Our Extra-Terrestrial brother is not an angel, neither is he a Saint of God. He is a very natural human being who has arrived where he is by a process of evolution – evolution by trial and error – over immensities of time and, very probably, through a multitude of different life-experiences. So we speculate, but this is, after all, the religious belief of men and women concerning life on this Earth and is, arguably, an application to present circumstances of that which yet stirs in the deep memory.

Trial, error, honest misjudgement and their resulting calamities are not serious moral issues in that they seldom damage the integrity of those concerned – though they may well threaten their present lives and well-being. Our Extra-Terrestrial brother has probably suffered much in his growth to wherever he is but, I suggest, he has not suffered the unique calamity of identification with an objectively malign Principle which is both other than himself and prior to himself in Creation.

The Incarnation may thus have a far wider significance and application than orthodox Earthly religious understanding allows. The restoration to unity of the Total Creature, Mankind, involved the rescue of that part of it which had become detached, deranged, lost altogether to the rest. But *Incarnation cannot be other than a re-Creation of the Creature;* Earthly Man is *other* than his brethren as a result of it and is raised, from the depths, to the heights of a *wholly new and wholly other* potential.

I suggest that we are now challenged to think it possible that what the Incarnation has accomplished on Earth has an application which is truly Cosmic, truly Universal. Fallen and redeemed Mankind – Mankind in Christ – partakes ever more fully than even our poetry can express, of what we understand as the Eternal High Priesthood of Christ. Fallen and redeemed Earthly Man in Christ – *The New Humanity* – is both priest and evangelist to his Extra-Terrestrial brethren!

A HIGHLY UNFASHIONABLE VIEW

All that has been suggested is utterly remote from our obsessions with "Star Wars" and the projection on to a newly-imagined stage of all our conditionings in mutual self-destruction. The world of "Space Fiction," with its heroes and heroines living brittle, mechanistic lives in "futuristic" settings, forever fighting off unimaginable dangers from without as well as drearily familiar dangers from within, bears no relation whatsoever to the vision here suggested.

By the same token, all our remarkable achievements in Space Technology, such as landing men on the Moon, sending television cameras to far-flung planets and landing robots on Mars, tend to confirm us in our own conditioning. The Mars upon which the robot has landed *must* be the only Mars there is! And yet it is only the Mars we know as it exists on that "wavelength," that plane of being, which we ourselves occupy.

Manned Exploration of the Solar System, beyond the Moon which is a satellite of the Earth, is a dream, a vision, an obsession. It is fuelled by profound stirrings in the depth of Earthly Mankind's being. It represents a desperate search for life, even though that life might now be extinct. It also represents a determination *not* to be alone in a meaningless Universe, even if not being alone involves the colonisation of other bodies, however inhospitable, in order that there are others, somewhere, not to be alone with, even on our own terms!

The effort, the dedication and the inventive genius involved is as heroic as it is absurd. The absurdity, however, is something that cannot be faced for the vision must be maintained until the bitter end, lest that end should prove to be the bitter end indeed!

CHAPTER NINE

THE extensive and all-embracing programmes of medical experiments, planning and calculation necessary to deliver two or three human beings to the planet Mars, sustain them during their stay, and return them in safety, raises a great many profound questions. One of the questions must concern the apparent ability of our Extra-Terrestrial brethren to actually do what they appear to be doing.

DEPENDENCE UPON EXTERNALS

Do our Extra-Terrestrial friends deteriorate, physically, in a prolonged condition of weightlessness? What regimes are necessary in order to keep them able to function normally and efficiently? And what of their environmental and natural life-support requirements? How are these transported? How does a Extra-Terrestrial relate to the Earthly environment? We know none of the answers to these questions. Speculation alone can give us a start, even to thinking about them.

I suggest that, among the many things that may surprise our Extra-Terrestrial brethren about us, it is our obvious *dependence upon externals* for sustenance that will predominate. Our normal and natural functions of eating and drinking are, I suggest, completely foreign to them! And our obvious dependence upon Earth's atmosphere, as it exists at more or less ground level, will probably astonish them! We may, perhaps, find in a slightly wider interpretation of the Adam and Eve myth, a clue to our very different circumstances in the fact that Adam, an exile from Paradise, is now dependent upon "the sweat of his brow" for survival.

In the mythological Paradise from which they were expelled, Adam and Eve were sustained *gratis*, by the very energies that brought them into being; their lives were supported by Life itself. After their Fall, their lives became precariously dependent upon what they could find to prey upon. They had suffered *a fall from species!* This is mythology, but myth conveys truths that lie buried in the deep memory and cannot be articulated in prose. We are, I suggest, the "odd ones out" among the wider family of Cosmic Humanity. Part, at least of our "oddity" may be seen in this extraordinary business of external, environmental life-support that we so evidently require and which so efficiently acts as a wall to our post-Paradisal prison.

CONCEPTIONS OF TIME AND SPACE

The next set of questions that must come into our minds include the following: What conception do our Extra-Terrestrial brethren have of Space? Of Time, measured in light-years? How long may some of them have been in the travelling and what is the relevance of their journeyings to a home-based society that they left – by our kind of understanding – years, decades, centuries or even millennia ago?

Once again, we know the answers to none of these questions. I suggest that our Extra Terrestrial brethren may have conceptions – and thus experiences – of Space, distance and duration that are quite other than our own. We use, as our yardstick of measurement, the speed of light. I suggest it possible that they may have another yardstick altogether: *the speed of thought!* Mind and mechanics are, I suggest, in the closest of partnerships among them and it is possible – even probable – that the actual mechanics are not identical as between our differing visiting groups.

I suggest that it is highly probable that our various visitors effect their journeys primarily *by thinking themselves where they want to be!* Their travels are likely to be *a collective exercise of mind in the first instance.* The mechanics, the technology involved, however sophisticated it might be, is as a pair of boots upon the feet of mind!

UNFASHIONABLE EVIDENCE TO HAND

In order to come to terms with the possibility of thought-guidance, even propulsion by means of concentrated thought, it is necessary to turn once more to that third discipline which is known to us as the occult. It is only fair to acknowledge that there is a great deal less secrecy – and in consequence a great deal less that is "occult" or "hidden" – in occult circles than there was a generation ago and, consequently, a great deal more is known about its concerns. Mind control and all the less-than-common human phenomena are all grist to this mill and, in these circles it is not considered either impossible or extraordinary that a human being can project himself, or herself, out of the body. The "out-of-body experience" is indeed in some danger of becoming respectable; a widely acknowledged – if as yet unexplained – fact of life.

It is worth our while to recognise that the "out of body" experience – and ability to induce it – is not confined to some esoteric underworld. Friends of the author, pillars of orthodoxy and of the most reassuring respectability, have described this experience to him, frequently and in detail.

One man who, later in life, was ordained to the priesthood, remembers, as a teenager, regularly projecting himself out of his body upon hearing the postman at the door in the morning. He would arrive at the front door, survey the envelopes lying on the door-mat, and then return to his bedroom and look at himself lying in bed before returning to his body. Years later, he was in the habit of projecting himself great distances in order to check up on the wellbeing of his ageing parents. As soon as he saw them going safely about their daily business, he would return, in an instant, to his body which was thousands of miles away on the other side of the world. He thought everybody did this kind of thing!

As my friend grew in maturity and wisdom, it came to him that this kind of invasion of his parents' privacy was not acceptable, however well intentioned. He also began to discern the dangers inherent in the practice and laid it aside as an ever present threat to his integrity.

A young woman, also a devout Christian believer, from time to time projected herself into her boyfriend's office and peered over his shoulder to see what he was doing. It was innocently intended, but he became aware of her presence and challenged her about it. She too realised the near-impossibility of using this, as a natural gift, without risk to her integrity.

A young girl suffered much unjust punishment for "telling lies," both from her parents and from her school matron. When she was obliged to change schools, the matron of the new school recognised what was happening; the girl was projecting out of her body, on to another plane or "close wavelength" and innocently describing her completely genuine adventures to adults who seemed to be incapable of hearing the truth when it was told to them! She had no idea that this was other than completely normal; she assumed everybody did it! Sixty years later, whenever a certain well-known river is mentioned, she still has to ask herself: "Which one? The ordinary one or the *other* one?"

Another young man, gifted in this way and well known to the author, was propositioned by a similarly gifted young woman who was attracted to him. Why, she asked, did they not meet out of the physical body for their assignations? He became alarmed at the multi-faceted dangers to wholeness and integrity that this might entail and politely declined! He had not the slightest doubts as to the feasibility of the proposal – none whatsoever!

However rare, and however inhibited this gift might be on Earth, and more particularly in sophisticated societies, it is a world-wide phenomenon: in some of the more primitive cultures it is deeply venerated, and in some occult circles – which take the less well known human faculties very seriously – attempts are made to cultivate it. Its use in the Natural Order, on Earth, is however fraught with very real dangers, both in the execution, *and to the integrity of a human will which is never without a measure of corruption, or of compromise*. Earthly temptations are such that its use must, sooner or later, be for advantage, profit, competition or for power.

What has been referred to must be regarded as – potentially at least – a normal function of natural humanity for which there must exist proper and natural contexts. I suggest that the comparative rarity among us of the gift of out-of-the-body projection is an indication of a de-rating of the Earthly human mind, its governing down, so that certain possible functions do not prove catastrophic to a compromised and partially corrupted human will.

The suggestion here made is that there is evidence enough upon Earth to indicate the possibility of thought-powered travel by a process of projection. We must then ask ourselves: Do our Extra-Terrestrial brethren therefore leave themselves at home and travel, in groups, by out-of-the-body projection? We do not know the answer to that question but I suggest that the answer is that, very probably, they do not. The mental mechanisms in minds uncomplicated by the Earthly human condition may very well make travel at the speed of thought, by means of the concentration of a group of minds, a possibility when allied to a technology that can give effect to the common intention. I suggest that such a technology – which may manifest in a number of different forms – will be found to be sophisticated more in its simplicity than in its complexity.

RECAPITULATION

We must return, briefly, to a consideration of ways and means of life-support, for our Extra-Terrestrial brethren appear to enjoy a greater liberty in these respects than we might expect for ourselves. I suggest, therefore, that they are probably sustained, not by anything external to them such as food, drink or atmosphere, but rather by the Cosmic Energy, the Divine Will, the Cosmic Life Force – call it what you will – that both creates and maintains all things in being.

Our Extra-Terrestrial brethren therefore, in all probability, neither eat, drink nor breathe; they are, like ourselves, each one a created human consciousness expressed (or manifested, if that word is preferred) in physical being. For us this is an animal business as well as a human one but I suggest that, typically, humanity is not animal at all and that the Earthly human condition is, in this respect, quite aberrational.

This being the case – if indeed it is the case – then the greatest single obstacle to our Extra-Terrestrial brethren's interstellar travel (however they understand or experience it) is overcome in that it never existed in the first place. The possibility of travel by some form of "thought-propulsion," and at the speed of thought, removes the second, virtually insuperable, obstacle, and we are left with a problem, trivial by comparison with the other two: that of the technology which is apparently necessary to the accomplishment of their missions and the fulfilment of their intentions.

CHAPTER TEN

AMONG the many other-than-terrestrial visitors to our own Earth there have been some who are entirely unconnected with all that has hitherto been discussed in these pages. They are quite unconnected with the Unidentified Flying Object or with any of the speculatively conceived technology associated with visitations from "outer space." Indeed, by comparison with these other visitors, our Extra-Terrestrial brethren hitherto considered resemble somewhat industrious and inquisitive next-door-neighbours.

ALTERNATIVE UNIVERSES

The idea of the Alternative Universe, or of other Universes altogether in addition to our own, is one that surfaces from time to time in the pages of Science Fiction. Like all imaginative writings, this *genre* imagines only what is possible to exist, for the inherently impossible is beyond the possibility of imagination. I suggest that the probable existence of entire Universes additional to, and quite other than, our own need neither surprise us nor threaten us. That their inhabitants might occasionally succeed in visiting us might fairly be felt as a surprise, but as nothing that is possible is impossible, the possibility can be quite readily accepted by a mind brave enough to try!

In respect of one such Alternative, the means of access to ourselves appears to be quite "other." There are no "flying saucers," nor are there "space craft" of some alien form. There is instead *a kind of corridor* which opens between one Universe and another and which permits access *not so much to places as to people and the close environment of those people.*

We then discover that, through this corridor from the almost unimaginable, we are encountering human beings, but of a somewhat different order and whom, if a description be attempted, seem to live and move at a somewhat more leisurely pace, both than ourselves and also than the various Extra-Terrestrial brethren whom we encounter from our own Universe.

The purpose of these visitations? I suggest that they are inspired by a general sense of the Convergence of things. That the time for coming together is upon both them and us, and that Time itself is perceived as being short.

Two questions must arise in our minds: Do all these visitors of ours know each other? To what extent is their pattern of visitation "orchestrated" and, if so, by whom?

I suggest that the answer to the first question may be both *Yes* and *No*. It may well be that visitors from other Universes than our own may be as startled as we are by all the evidence there is of Extra-Terrestrial visitation! Needless to say, we do not know. We do not know any more than we know how many alternative Universes we may be having dealings with!

As to the "orchestration" of all this visitation; I suggest that it might be said to operate upon three levels. The first and fundamental level is that which proceeds from the very heart of The Mystery in which all things – all Universes – abide. *A fundamental dynamic of convergence* is, I suggest, moving the totality of Cosmic Humanity. Here it is necessary that we remind ourselves that The Incarnation has not only to do with Earthly humanity but rather with the total Human Creature, Cosmos-wide and at every level. This is what is meant by the re-Creation, the New Heaven and the New Earth.

The second level of "orchestration" is by what we can only refer to as Heaven, the "Wholly Other" plane of being which both is and is becoming. If the first level represents God Himself, this second level is represented by His Angels and His Saints.

And there is a third level of "orchestration" which is to be found operating among our Extra-Terrestrial brethren. We ourselves are outside the sphere of its operations, for Earthly humanity, fallen, corrupted, redeemed and identified with the Crucified and Risen Incarnate Lord, falls directly – and through no merits of its own – under the "orchestrating" direction of Heaven.

PART THREE

An Exercise in Absurdity:
A Thought Thinks the Mind

PROLOGUE TO PART THREE

What now follows must be regarded, by all rational people, as an exercise in the absurd. Only a fool would contemplate it, for how can a creature presume to pontificate upon the ambience of Creation as a whole? How can a thought proceed to expand upon the nature of the Mind that thinks it?

The Essence of The Mystery is unknowable, and it can only be "known" and experienced in terms of the Energies proceeding from the Essence. What follows, therefore, must have to do with Energies as experienced rather than with the Essence which is beyond knowing. All, therefore, is metaphor, and I suggest, all is Mind.

*Mind is, perhaps, a metaphor for Mystery
and all is mind, and Mind is manifest
in myriad minds, each one the energy
of its unique and given essence. All gift,
and gift itself an energy, the energy
of Essence inconceivable. So minds must seek
their meaning, must fulfil their fundamental quest
of self-forgetting. All is mind, and mind creates
by thinking thoughts, and thoughts are things
made manifest, complete with being, all bestowed.*

*Love manifests in creatures. Love creates;
The Mystery is Love, the "how" and "why."
This is our experience. This Love, it incarnates.
What knows a well-frog of the bright blue sky?*

CHAPTER ELEVEN

BETWEEN ourselves and Reality there lies what we might describe as an intermediate zone, a transforming and translating agency, or mechanism, which interprets Reality to us in terms which are humanity-relatable in one way or another. Not for nothing did the Hebrew of the Old Testament believe that to see the face of God was instantly fatal! Connect a bicycle lamp directly to the high tension wires overhead and all you are left with is molten metal, a charred corpse and an all-pervading smell of burning.

LIVING BY METAPHOR

Like it or not, we live by metaphor. We perceive in terms of metaphor. The very Creeds of Holy Church are catalogues of holy and most faithful metaphors, for what they are able to suggest is always unimaginably greater than what they are able to articulate. They resemble the scribble drawings of a small child's perceptions of things. They are the best we can do, being what we are.

Mind itself is, perhaps, the most faithful metaphor of all which is available to us of *The Mystery itself*. We know Mind is only metaphor and not the Reality which it suggests to us because our own minds tell us so. But Mind and our own minds have everything in common. Mind is a metaphor but it is also sacramental, an Icon. The understanding of, and participation in, the Universal Mind (however fractionally) in which every creature that exists is a thought, is as it were the inwardly-outward, just comprehensible *sign* of The Mystery which both contains it and indwells it and is, we might say, its inward and spiritual *grace*. It is also an icon, a picture consecrated for the Divine indwelling.

THE CREATION OF WORLDS AND THEIR CREATURES

The mind of every mortal man, woman and child is full of self-created worlds within which quite a large proportion of their own lives are lived. There is no shortage of space within the human mind, for its capacity is infinite and only a small portion of its earthly vehicle, the brain, is ever fully activated.

The human mind has no difficulty in principle in the creation of an entire Universe within itself – indeed several Universes – organising them, peopling them and providing them with both a past and a future as well as a present moment. The works of fiction writers in any *genre* are evidence enough of this, but it is an activity that any child can engage in and untold multitudes do so. Indeed it may be argued that it is exactly this natural ability and disposition which makes us truly human; both image and likeness of Mind itself, as Holy Scripture maintains.

The human faculty of the imagination is that which creates images. It provides a kind of interior-flesh-and-blood manifestation within the mind. This is prior to any artifact that the human hands might then proceed to make, thus inspired. The inner is therefore always prior to the outer and seldom indeed does the outer manifestation – the artifact – live up to its interior promise. When it does, it is – whatever it is – a work of art for, as such, it is able to communicate something of the primary intuition that created it to other human minds.

A MATTER OF SCALE

In human terms only, Mind contains in Timelessness every human mind that has ever existed, together with every one of their own thoughts and imaginings. The capacity of Mind, therefore, is – in a rather child-like exercise in mathematics – somewhat in excess of infinity multiplied by infinity! There is ample room, therefore, for an infinitude of worlds, planes of being, dimensions, wavelengths – or what you will – upon every one of which entire Universes may manifest. Our problem, therefore, in coming to terms with the unthinkable and entirely unimaginable "greater environment" in which we and all things exist might be compared to that of the well-frog who, as a Chinese saying points out, has a somewhat limited experience and comprehension of the sky.

I suggest that, when all our purely intellectual strivings fail in frustration and exhaustion, we do well to allow phenomena to simply be what they appear to be. Our Extra-Terrestrial brother is best accepted at face value, as is the so-far puzzling vehicle in which he appears to travel.

Mortal, earthly man observes a limitless Universe and attempts to imagine the immensities of Outer Space, as it appears to him and as he understands it. The exercise is quite self-defeating but it is nevertheless compelling. In another mental pigeon-hole, however, there lies an awareness that all these unimaginable physical immensities, both of his own Earth and of every other heavenly body, are lined at every point with what can best be described as a psychic *within*. Indeed everything he can see is the expression, the manifestation in physical terms, of its own *interior* reality.

The *within* of the Universe is prior to the *without*. I suggest that it is also incomparably more vast. The term "Inner Space" is variously used. Sometimes it is used with reference to the ultra-miniscule, sub-atomic universe which is as limitless in one direction as the visible Universe is in the other. Perhaps related to this use of the term, but altogether transcending it, is that "Inner Space" which is the psychic *within* of the very Universe itself. This is, supremely, the realm of Mind.

The psychic *within* of Earth itself is more than the earthly human mind can cope with but it is, needless to say, contained within, and altogether transcended by, the Inner Space within which the essences and realities of creatures display their own energies in the first instance. The matter might be summed up somewhat as follows:

> *The Inner Planes are part of Inner Space,*
> *contained, as is this outer Earth, to line*
> *earth's each dimension and at every point.*
>
> *The Inner Space transcends, contains*
> *the Outer; is dimensionless and other, and beyond;*
> *and is the proper ambience of Contemplation.*
>
> *The Inner Planes of Outer Earth*
> *are bounded by its aura. Here the mind*
> *can reach, and this the realm of Meditation.*
>
> *Yet inner Space transcends it all, directionless.*
> *The heart is Man's own lodestone, and who yearns*
> *beyond imagining shall touch God's own imagination.*

NOT COSMOLOGY BUT CREATIVITY

No cosmology is offered in these pages, rather the reverse. All knowledge is, in the end, but working hypothesis and is applicable only where – and if – it works. The incomprehensibility of the totality of things is here celebrated, together with the delight of being able to discover what needs to be known, for we live, and are informed, on a "need to know" basis.

Mind is our metaphor for The Mystery. Our own minds participate in Mind for they are made by it, in its own image and likeness, specifically so to participate. The primary characteristic of Mind – and our own minds – is creativity, and love for creatures is the underlying motivation and dynamic. Through creativity, we creative minds engage in the process of becoming what we are, of realising the potential of each individual's being. Mind is, one might say, both full-bodied and full-blooded; its vigour extends in every direction and upon every plane of being, every dimension and wavelength. Governed down though our mortal, earthly minds might seem to be, nevertheless they too function naturally and best when fully engaged on all the levels available to them. Thus an intellectualism which rejects all that its own two-dimensional world-view cannot contain is both bloodless and partial.

Mind can change; indeed it is of the very nature of mind that it changes but, unless there is something perverse or pathological about it, the changes will always be congruous with what has gone before. The thoughts of Mind develop and there is always the possibility of a New Idea which, in the context of the Mind of All, is likely to mean a New Creation.

> "Now I am making the whole of creation new." *(Rev 21: 5)*

> "Then I saw a new heaven and a new earth; the first heaven and the first earth had disappeared..." *(Rev 21: 1)*

CREATION RE-LAUNCHED

The life of the imagination in any normal man, woman or child assures us that, within the Divine Imagination, there is infinite room for a whole

New Creation in which the old is summed up, tidied up, fulfilled and re-launched with a new beginning and an infinitude of new and hitherto unimagined possibilities. Are these new and unimagined possibilities hitherto unimagined by very Mind itself? Who can say? But we are at liberty to treat them as if this were the case, whatever the unknowable-by-us case may be.

Our hard-and-fast, pigeon-hole categories are already inadequate on their own for none are big enough, on their own. Religion, secure in its pigeon-hole in isolation from the other disciplines of life, and in meaningless competition with them, loses both its relevance to daily life and, in consequence, its vigour. It fast degenerates into a collection of holy-clubs, or pietistic-observance-societies for the like-minded on the one hand, and an academic desert of "theologies of concepts" and philosophies of religion on the other. Its Institutions become increasingly dedicated to self-preservation. Their hierarchies become increasingly preoccupied with power and influence and with matters of money.

Science, trying to exist in isolation from the "non-scientific," remains at a soulless nuts and bolts level, however sophisticated its technology may become. It must, I suggest, escape from its pigeon-hole and look beyond itself towards the "*Why?*" as well as properly concerning itself with the "*How?*" It is no accident that the modern mystic is as likely to be a physicist as a religious contemplative. The style may differ, but The Mystery has claimed them both.

By the same token, occultism must abandon *the Occult*, for the "occult" is, blessedly, fast losing its "hiddenness." More and more of its concerns are opening up to the scientist on the one hand, and to the laterally thinking religionist on the other. It is also becoming a commonplace that there is not, and never was, such a thing as "The Supernatural." All things are of Nature and are Natural, but Nature exists upon a myriad planes of being, wavelengths and dimensions.

Awareness of this state of affairs, and acceptance of it, is fast becoming the common ground of the Religionist, the Scientist and the Occultist, though entrenched positions, and the fear which binds men and women to them, will resist the advance of the obvious to the bitter end.

But Nature, at whatever level, is perfected, transformed, transfigured and re-launched in a New Creation by the Divine Grace.

And what is the Divine Grace but the re-creating dynamic of The Mystery – Ultimate Person and the source of all personhood – working within creatures in a total Creation which is *wholly personal* because it can be none other?

CHAPTER TWELVE

To describe Creation as infinite is hardly to do it justice. Every created mind creates, and the sum of all that the myriad minds have ever created is still very far from the sum of things. Mind participates in all created minds, just as created minds participate in Mind. To a limited extent, and usually at the subconscious levels, created minds participate in each other. There is, as it were, a process of *osmosis* between created minds. Each mind, however, has an integrity and an autonomy of its own and thus mutual participation is appropriately limited.

ALL CREATURES MODIFY EACH OTHER

An inevitable consequence of the above is that all creatures are, to a limited degree, creations of each other. Person A's perceptions of Person B are, to a large degree, subjective. In the eyes of A, therefore, that other will not be the B that actually exists but rather "b" who is the creation of A's perceptions of B. That creation will then be projected on to B who will then be, to some small degree, modified by it. A deepening relationship between A and B will result in a gradual modification of the perceived "b" in the direction of the true original.

Needless to say, the same process will take place in the opposite direction and so, while A is relating, in the first instance, to "b," B will be similarly relating to "a." The fulfilment of their relationship will be the mature friendship of "A (modified by B)" and "B (modified by A)" and both modifications will be, ideally, in the direction of the fulfilment both of the "A-hood" and of the "B-hood." A happy marriage is an admirable illustration of this.

The observed is always modified by the observer, and the observer is likewise modified by the observed. Absolute detachment and objectivity is impossible for created minds. It must remain a matter for conjecture (and not for dogmatism) as to its absolute possibility for Mind Itself, for:

> *The Word was made flesh,*
> *he lived among us,*

and, even more remarkably:

> *What proves that God loves us*
> *is that Christ died for us*
> *while we were still sinners.* (**Romans 8:8**)

We may, perhaps, sum up as follows, for we are all sinners – though redeemed:

> *All things exist within the Mind alone,*
> *thus you exist in me, and I in you,*
> *and both within the Mind which thinks us two.*
> *We think the thoughts that Mind has thought*
> *and clothe them with our images. Thus you*
> *are clothed by me, and I by you*
> *with some quite other being than our own*
> *which, like our own, is not our own*
> *but given. And thus we play at being God*
> *and get it wrong. The Mind, the Mind alone*
> *bestows the Real upon its thoughts, and we,*
> *neglecting paradox, stoke up the fires.*
> *All ego-driven by illusory desires,*
> *we play the fool; frustrate in fantasy!*

Creation is both perpetual and in perpetual modification, for every creature is a modifying agency for every other creature and, in this, we might claim to see some at least of the thinking processes of Mind Itself revealed. This, however, is an almightily grand, sweeping statement for any creature to make, to whom every second modifying influence is pleasurable and the rest are painful!

The evolutionary process, both of and within species, is evidence enough of the modifying influence of that other multitude of creatures whom we conveniently lump together and call "the environment." The balances are fine, however, and disproportionate actions will produce equally disproportionate reactions. Both, in their own way, are painful and excessively modifying influences upon all other creatures affected. Environmental damage and pollution, and their consequences for living creatures on every level, are evidence enough of this.

It is very easy, however, to become stuck in the mud of specific issues and concerns. We are here concerned to proclaim that very mud itself, however muddy, is mind-stuff. All is mind and all is, in its own way, part of a semi-autonomous thought-pattern within Mind Itself

THE LORD OF THE DANCE

The Marseilles Tarot, deeply respected by students of occult lore and regarded – quite mistakenly – as devilish by some kinds of religionist, exhibits a truly remarkable insight into some at least of the archetypal forces of creation as they are experienced by Earthly men and women. The profundity of insight, and the potency of symbol – a matter with which we shall deal on a later page – means that the misguided and the manipulative can misuse what the Tarot puts into their hands. Any fault, however, lies in the misuser, not in the thing misused.

Of the twenty-two Trump Cards (from which the Court Cards in a conventional pack of playing cards are a pale derivative), twenty-one are numbered in a deliberate sequence. The un-numbered Trump Card (sometimes numbered Zero) is called *The Fool*. It depicts a cheerful tramp, with a bundle and stick over his shoulder, who is apparently entirely unconcerned that a small dog has just torn the seat from his trousers! This Tarot Trump represents The Mystery, Mind Itself. He is the Lord of the Cosmic Dance.

I wander through the Mind of God,
Says God, with tattered breeks; unclassified.
Dogs snap at my heels, and all
That I have made is most magnificent;
Rejoices in its being. That is good,
Says God, for so we all rejoice together.

And as I wander with my bundle and stick,
Says God, the endless dance is danced
And I pass the time of day, and dance,
And let my creatures carry me away.

> *Such is my courtship. I am everywhere and yet –*
> *Unclassified, with tattered breeks – preside.*
>
> *I have made all this from my rib,*
> *Says God. A fool am I for Love,*
> *And represent myself to mine*
> *For love of mine. And mine reflect*
> *Us both! You doubt my style of deity?*
> *Ah! But I'm unclassified! A fool! Says God.*

I suggest that the capacity of men and women to project themselves on to the middle of their own mental stage may constitute as good an image of Mind Itself as we are likely to find. We are all to be found performing in the midst of our own creations. We have a relationship with our own thoughts which, in sum, do not constitute the totality of ourselves any more than the thoughts in the Eternal Mind constitute to totality of the Creator. Monism, naked and unadorned, fails us, both microcosmically and macrocosmically alike.

Treading the boards of our own mental stage, we are perpetually to be discovered in situations, domestic, work or leisure, which are entirely imaginary. We relate to real people – but as we imagine them, projecting our imaginations upon them – all within our own heads. We conduct both feuds and romances within our own heads, usually of an incredible ferocity and intensity, and we ourselves occupy centre-stage throughout.

I project my own subjective self on to the centre of my mental stage and take the leading role in all my inner dramas, comedies, tragedies, romances and soap-operas. Being but human and very fallible, I am at once heroic, romantic, entirely admirable and supremely righteous in all my roles! So, I venture to suggest, are we all! This is an activity that goes on within the mind of every man, woman and child there is, ever was or ever will be. *It images the mental activity of Mind Itself.* We are made in the likeness of Mind Itself.

Of what, then, is this the image? I suggest that it is the image of the way in which the Creator of All projects His subjective Self on to the centre of his own mental stage and lives in perpetual relationship with ourselves and all other creatures, who are His thoughts. Thus what we might presume to call the subjective Self of our Creator (The Logos,

The Word, The Eternal Son of God) is objective to us, known to us, experienced by us. And in The Incarnation of this subjective Self:

we saw his glory,
the glory that is his as the only Son of the Father,
full of grace and truth.

and also,

It is the same God that said, "let there be light shining out of darkness," who has shone in our minds to radiate the light of the knowledge of God's glory, the glory on the face of Christ." (2 Cor 4: 6)

This is what the description *The Lord of the Dance* means, used of Christ who is both Cosmic and Incarnate. In a different tradition altogether, one of the Hindu understandings of Deity is represented by Siva, dancing on the heads of the demons, at the centre of the Universe in his own capacity as Lord of the Dance.

The Fool, the Anti-hero, the Lord of the Dance, are images of Christ which have been pushed aside in favour of the equally and profoundly truthful images of the tragic and the triumphal. That this is so reflects, I suggest, our very urgent Earthly perspectives and may even reflect, unconsciously, some rather worldly priorities as well. We are uneasy about "the foolishness of God" and we prefer the heroic to the anti-heroic. We prefer, therefore, to concentrate almost entirely upon Christ Crucified. We then go on to concentrate upon Christ Risen, Ascended, Glorified. Somewhat perversely, we are more at ease doing it this way!

In much the same way, we give all our devotional attention to The Incarnation and forget about the Cosmic Christ, whom both St Paul and St John are at extreme pains to proclaim, lest we do what we are inclined to do – lose sight of *The Wood* for The Tree of Glory! Others, who might feel quite at ease with the idea of "incarnations" but are made uneasy by the reality of The Incarnation and its demands, are happy to keep Christ Cosmic for fear that He should ever actually touch ground!

The Apocryphal New Testament book, *The Acts of John*, concludes with an account of the Last Supper which adds a dimension to the accounts in the Canonical Gospels. At the end of the meal, the disciples are formed into a circle, holding hands, with our Lord stood in the middle. They are to answer *Amen* to what He sings, and then they are to dance round Him to His singing.

This is, of course, The Cosmic Dance with The Lord of the Dance both presiding and dancing with the dancers. The song touches upon the meaning of the Incarnation and upon the dance of the Cosmos about its Lord. In the middle of this Hymn of Jesus, there come the words:

> *I will be thought,*
> *Being wholly thought.*

which, in another translation, is rendered more accessibly as:

> *I am Mind of All!*
> *Fain would I be known.*

To which the dancing disciples, and the present writer, respond with the words "So be it," or, in the original Hebrew, *Amen!*

CHAPTER THIRTEEN

Both space and time are metaphors of Mystery,
concomitants of creaturehood, coordinates of form
and Love's own limits to the limitless,
contained within both Uncreated and created mind.

Thus space and time are both transcended quite
as each created mind, in its own timelessness,
by Grace gives back its gift and penetrates the Mystery;
the Mind of Grace transcending, re-creating mind.

And thus is metaphor the context of our creaturehood
who hold in being by the Uncreated Light
shone deep within, to light up our first cause
and first causation – thought of us within the Mind
beyond all mind, set deep within the Uncreate.
And yet we still bewail our transient state!

THE object of our current study is to make an attempt to grasp something of an understanding, however fleeting, however slight, of what we might describe as the Ultimate Environment in which all things exist. This is a mould-breaking rather than a mould-making exercise for I suggest that we are in some need of liberation from the almost inescapable tendency to accept the world – indeed the Universe – as we see it, experience it, weigh it and measure it, as Absolute. All is Mind; that is our liberation. We know it, deep within ourselves, but the pressures of the visible and the physical are all but overwhelming.

We are engaged in an attempt to fit the Extra-Terrestrial into our time-space system as it is experienced by us in our everyday lives; within this world with its telescopes, microscopes, saws, hammers and nails. But our dear brother, the Extra-Terrestrial, doesn't fit! And yet some of us have encountered him and more still have seen – or are reasonably convinced that we have seen – the vehicles in which he travels. He appears and disappears from our radar screens; he is "picked up," and then lost again, by various forms of instrumentation. We are tempted – even encouraged by certain interest-groups – to conclude that "he can't exist, therefore he doesn't exist, and the man who says he does exist is mad and should be offered counselling and early retirement!" But this is blatant evasion of a pressing issue and one not, perhaps, conspicuous either for its courage or its honesty.

Our current study has to do with the Extra-Terrestrial. We are maintaining that All is Mind and, in so doing, it is necessary sometimes to arise (some would say, descend!) to poetry in order to suggest what cannot be adequately articulated in prose.

COORDINATES AND BRIDGING THE DIMENSIONAL GAPS
Time and space provide a continuum within which creatures can objectify into existence. What begins as an idea becomes concrete, time and space being parts of the process of concretion. Outer space, so called is, I suggest, the space necessary for a pattern of thoughts, of possibilities, to come into manifestation, to become tangible, to become concrete. The time element in the case of the visible Universe is as meaningless to Earthly mortal man as the space element is unimaginable. All creatures, all planes of being, dimensions, wavelengths or what you will, have their own time-space coordinates. When conscious minds meet, each from a different time-space continuum, it is necessary that there be established what we can best describe as a *bridging continuum* in order that the encounter may be effected. I suggest that the formation of bridging continua is a normal function of Nature which is activated to meet circumstances as they arise.

I make so bold as to suggest that the state of fulfilment, consummation and re-creation, to which we give the name Heaven, also has its time-space coordinates, or their equivalents, without which Heaven and the Heavenly could not *be*. The bridging continua are here much in evidence within the context of mystical prayer and revelation. (Among the latter, the most obvious examples are the various initiatives undertaken by the Mother of God at Lourdes, Knock, Fatima and Zeitoun, to mention but a few.) I suggest that there are few persons on this Earth who have not had some experience of this kind of bridging continuum, in one form or another, however fleetingly, however misinterpreted.

It is necessary to remember that "the bridge," upon which conscious minds meet and relate one to another, is *quite other* than either of the "banks" upon which its two ends are set. It is but a bridge, a creation of Mind and of minds, and it is variously decorated and adorned, usually very subjectively. Its function, however, could hardly be more objective.

The question now arises as to what kinds of bridging continua are necessary to enable our encounters with the Extra-Terrestrial to take place? This question is neither easy to answer nor even to ask for a completely different *character of encounter* is here experienced. Psychic perception can sometimes relate to Earthly humans in an apparently Earth-bound post-mortem state, or indeed in a variety of such states. Magic constructs its own, man-made bridging continua (the telesmatic image) in order to be able to relate to, and communicate with its "Inner Plane Adepti," an essentially *Inner Planes of Earth* field of concern.

We have already made mention of the more usual kind of bridging continuum, that which enables the Heavenly and the Earthly mortal consciousness to relate. With the Extra-Terrestrial, however, we have something that is quite *other*.

It is *other* because our Extra-Terrestrial brethren are living in the very same life-state as we ourselves. They are neither post-mortem in some species of Paradise or Purgatory, nor are they Heavenly beings. They are most decidedly "of the Earth, earthy," except that they appear to belong, not to Planet Earth on any of its planes of being, but to a selection of other, so far unidentified, equivalent "Earths" existing on another wavelength or dimension than our own.

We encounter our Extra-Terrestrial brethren either in apparent physical form *as if* on our own wavelength and seen with our own physical eyes, or our encounters take place on a bridging continuum which involves inner vision and its equivalent in the other senses. (I suggest that those *most physically* encountered – for want of a better way of putting it – may be humanoid rather than fully human.) We see what we see, and glimpse what we glimpse with inner vision rather than with outer – though sometimes, fleetingly, with both. The "sense of presence" can be very strong indeed and it is possible, if sufficiently recollected and unalarmed oneself, to "pick up" emotions such as apprehension (theirs, not ours!), relief, warmth and – best of all – affection.

It is also possible, sometimes, to engage the sense of touch. Once trust and acceptance are assured and all fear and apprehension have departed, it is a most moving experience to feel the hand of an Extra-Terrestrial brother in one's own hand, or his friendly grasp of one's own forearm.

MEETINGS OF MINDS

Communication takes place between minds, all of which are participators in Mind. In the case of communication with the Extra-Terrestrial, it takes place in a manner generally referred to as telepathic. There are, however, a great many different kinds of telepathic communication, and at many different levels. Suffice it for the present that *essential meaning* is transmitted from mind to mind and that each mind articulates that essential meaning for itself, in its own mode of articulation. There is a meeting of very similar minds in any unfearful encounter between Earthly and Extra-Terrestrial humans. Personal relationships can soon be established and mutual trust and confidence can be built up between the parties involved.

Our essential being, and the essential being of our Extra-Terrestrial brother, has a common source and origin in *the idea* of the Creature, Mankind which resides at the very heart of The Mystery. We are thus all *persons of the one Creature*, and as such we image our best understanding of that Divine Paradox of the very Mystery Itself: three Persons but one God. There is, therefore, a common created mind of which we are all partakers in that it is the Mind of the Creature, Mankind. Of this we shall have more to suggest on a later page.

Communication, therefore, is inherently possible, however opaque its mechanics may seem to our rationalistic and would-be sophisticated culture. Telepathic communication between minds, and its interpretation within receiving minds, is a commonplace.

Communication between Earthly and Extra-Terrestrial minds is a voyage of mutual discovery. There is much that is common to both and a great deal, in respect of experience and knowledge, that is peculiar to each. Both minds will encounter that which is hitherto outside their experience. In particular the Extra-Terrestrial will encounter in Earthly minds a deep seated sense of fear, and also the condition of paranoia which will be entirely foreign to him. The equally unexpected will also be discovered by ourselves in the Extra-Terrestrial mind.

The most immediate puzzle to the Extra-Terrestrial may be the close identity of Earthly Mankind with the environment and our dependence upon it. For us, the Earth itself possesses a spiritual dimension and we ourselves are aware of a responsibility for its proper management and well being – however unfaithful we may be to our innate vocation. The very idea of such dependence, such close spiritual as well as physical relationship with our environment may well seem quite foreign to him. The idea of eating and drinking is, I suggest, an astonishment to our brother and, not being dependent upon atmosphere for survival, his experience of the sense of sound will be quite other than our own.

There is much advantage in our Extra-Terrestrial brother being only fleetingly visible – if visible at all – to ourselves, however visible his vehicles might sometimes be. (I am not here referring to the small-statured Extra-Terrestrial humanoids who are sometimes as visible as they can be intrusive.) The encounter between persons is not distorted by subjective factors such as the shocks and surprises of unfamiliar appearance, though I suggest our Extra-Terrestrial brother is better able to see us than we are able to see him. It is possible for warmth, integrity and affection to establish a bond, for it is *person encountering person* and not two persons reacting to appearances.

WHAT ARE WE DOING HERE?

I suggest that the main interest that we excite in our Extra-Terrestrial brethren concerns some unexpected questions in their minds that would not occur in our own. What are we, their brethren, doing *here* on a plane of being (wavelength, dimension) otherwise uninhabited if not altogether uninhabitable? Why are we completely identified with an animal creation which is not our own order of being at all? What happened? And what might be the wider significance of it?

CHAPTER FOURTEEN

The myriad worlds that manifest in mind
are interwoven to beyond infinity. And so it is
within the minds of mortal men, and so
within the Mind of All. But men are blind
and locked within coordinates. They search the psyche,
its nature all contaminate, and worship what they find.

Cosmic calamity! The creature all turned in,
unable to proceed beyond its own within.
All separate from spirit, so the psyche spins
and spirals into vortices and out. No end
and no integrity, inhibited its powers
for Mind will only to the human spirit lend
its all-transcending faculties. So mortal man, and fallen, still
abides in isolation with his self-destroying will.

THE interpretation of Holy Scripture in order to fit a particular hypothesis is, almost always, a very doubtful undertaking. Special pleadings require arbitrary interpretations and it is not the intention of the present study to embark upon them. It is not out of order, however, to ask a few speculative questions, providing that their status is kept clear and that no ill-fitting answers are arbitrarily bolted on to the ends of them.

FOLK MEMORY

The influence of folk-memory in early Biblical mythology is clear and it is unarguable, save among the most determinedly literalist interpreters. Examples which spring most readily to mind include the Twelve Tribes of Israel, arguably an amphictyonic grouping of clans of a kind apparently common at that time and in that place. The Twelve Tribes merged their separate tribal mythologies into a common mythology.

The tribal patriarchs became the twelve sons of Israel in the process and all thus partook of a common heritage and mythology.

The Great Flood, and the mythological character of Noah, very probably reflects the folk memory of an ancient catastrophic inundation. There is some archeological evidence of such an event in the Tigris-Euphrates basin from which the Israelite tribes believed themselves to have come. The first Patriarch, Abraham, followed a well-known migration route, via the "fertile crescent," and there is ample archeological evidence of the patriarchal culture, with its customs and laws, spread across the fertile crescent from the Tigris-Euphrates basin into present-day Syria and Lebanon.

A people naturally defines itself in the first instance in terms of mythology rather than in terms of text-book-style history. Folk memories and their expression (and interpretation) in myth abound in every culture. There is also what might be described as a common folk memory, expressing itself differently in mythologies all over the world, concerning two linked and seemingly inseparable events. The first concerns the creation of mankind and the second concerns a calamity of cosmic dimensions whereby mankind, by its own fault, "falls through" or "falls out" or is cast out into some kind of exile. The expulsion of Adam and Eve from Paradise is but one of many such mythologies.

From a life of apparent ease, Adam and Eve were exiled to a situation in which life depended upon hard work to sustain it with food and drink, and with childbirth, animal style, becoming necessary for the continuance of the species. Perhaps we will not ask the speculative questions that begin to suggest themselves. Perhaps it is better simply to raise a quizzical eyebrow.

In passing, we might remember the "Lost Continent" of Atlantis and the astonishing hold that this has had on the imagination of a wide spectrum of people, provoking all manner of research and speculation, most of it fruitless. In short, Atlantis sank beneath the waves to the accompaniment of volcanic eruptions, so it is said, under the weight of its own wickedness.

THE SENSE OF ALIENATION

A common thread runs through the self-understanding of Earthly mankind, as it is variously expressed in the many cultures and religious systems of the world. It is an awareness of *disorder within* and that things are not as they should be. Lao-Tse, wearied by official corruption in the China of his day, contrasted the order of the Cosmos, and of its undergirding principle, with the disorder within mankind. "Look at the Cosmos and behave accordingly" is the burden of his teaching. In a later generation, Confucius sought to harmonise a disordered society by regulating the conduct of specific key relationships between persons. On the other side of the Himalayas, his contemporary, the Buddha, identified the principle of disorder as *desire* within the individual and taught his Noble Eightfold Path as the way to follow in order that desire may be quietened and eventually cease.

The Semitic tradition, along with many others (including, in part, the North American Indian) put forward mythologies of primary disobedience leading to a loss of integrity and exile. The Hebrew "Fall of Adam" is the supreme and most deeply thought-out example of this. Within the Christian tradition that sprang from the Hebrew, a developed doctrine of "Original Sin" followed, which among some Christians has become somewhat overdeveloped.

The Western Mystery Tradition of Kabbalistic Occultism makes reference to a "Prime Deviation" which closely follows a more conventional understanding of the nature of man, but with a somewhat different terminology.

The conventional, threefold, understanding of a human being as Spirit, Soul/Psyche and Body identifies the dis-integration as being "located" between the Spirit and the Soul/Psyche. Whereas the Body is intended to be the vehicle and physical earthly expression of both Spirit and Soul/Psyche, it is in fact at the mercy of a disordered Soul/Psyche at odds with itself and essentially out of touch with its own Spirit.

All these are working hypotheses and "ways of saying it." The working hypotheses work as adequately as any self-understanding can be expected to do. Religion, as I have already suggested, is the product of the sense of alienation, dis-integration and exile that this disturbed self-awareness produces in us. The Spiritual Quest is twofold; we seek God, from whom we feel separated, and we seek the re-integration of our total selves. These two strands are inseparable.

THE EFFECTS OF ALIENATION

Alienation and dis-integration from the spirit turns the Earthly human mind inwards upon itself The inner vision is thus concentrated upon the psyche and the psychic rather than upon the spirit and the spiritual. Confusion is the worse confounded by an inbuilt tendency to confuse the psychic for the spiritual and to direct worship to the created in confusion for the Creator. The psychic inner vision can only relate to things of Earth and the various wavelengths, dimension or planes of being of the Earth-state. *The inner worlds of exile are thus mistaken for what they are not.* The dis-integrated mind of Earthly man is Earthbound and can reach only fitfully beyond the limits that this state imposes.

Where, in this threefold model of spirit, soul/psyche and body, does the mind of man lie? The classical model is, needless to say, but a pencil sketch of a multi-faceted reality, however faithful it may be within its obvious limitations. The mind may best be understood as transcending – or, if you prefer, "lying behind" – the three levels of a human's being and it abides in a "governed down" state due to the dis-integration to which we have referred.

The human mind is thus unable to function normally, knowing and understanding on the "need to know" basis which is natural to all partakers in Mind, at whatever level. The spiritual quest, which lies at the heart of all the religions of the world, is for re-integration and, in the language of mythology, for re-admission to the Paradise from which Adam and Eve were exiled. This, I suggest, is a fruitless undertaking, for Mind does not run backwards; Mind does not turn the clock back.

Time may go forwards, backwards or sideways, but Mind, in whom all times and spaces abide, thinks in a myriad dimensions within the Eternal Now but it nevertheless *progresses*. The Garden of Eden is no longer there to be re-entered. All has progressed; Earthly man has altered almost beyond recognition and so has everything else. The religious quest, however faithful, however admirable, is entirely fruitless unless, or until, *some entirely new thinking* takes place within the Eternal Now of Mind Itself.

AN INHUMAN CONDITION

It is a natural, if less than admirable, human trait to project one's own faults and failings upon another. It is also natural to us Earthly mortals to attempt to involve others in our own errors, both in order to deflect attention from ourselves, and also to attempt – however absurdly – to establish an "alternative righteousness" to that from which one has lapsed. Any schoolboy or schoolgirl is familiar with this latter.

The myth of Adam and Eve illustrates these traits with all the vividness of a strip-cartoon. Adam, when found out, blames Eve for tempting him and making him eat the forbidden fruit – as if he had no mind or will of his own. Eve, the first to eat the forbidden fruit, bent all her powers to involve Adam in her own error, thus both hoping to hide behind him and also seeking – with a cosmic absurdity – to establish an "alternative normality" in which it was "OK" to eat forbidden fruit!

Every honest mortal can identify, with compassion and even with affection, with Adam and Eve in their disobedience, their weakness and their cowardice. We can also identify with Eve in her attempt to blame an influence *outside herself*, as if she too had neither mind nor will of her own. And yet the whole of Earthly humanity has been aware, for as long as can be traced, of a principle of disorder which seems to be *both exterior and interior* to mankind, and whose worst excesses manifest in and through human beings in their treatment of each other and of other creatures. A spirit of self-destruction lies at the heart of Earthly mankind. Paranoia rears its head at the slightest provocation and it may not be without significance in this context that Ego-driven competition – driven sometimes to lengths that are both pathological and destructive – comes everywhere more easily to us than self-effacing cooperation.

This state of affairs – of universal experience, together with the attempts of normal men and women to lead normal, happy lives in a normal society, despite tendencies to disorder both without and within – is *the human condition*.

I suggest that our Extra-Terrestrial brethren are disconcerted and sometimes disorientated upon entry to what can best be described as the Aura of Planet Earth. I also suggest that some at least of the deliberate contacts made with them by Earthly humans have caused them to experience, and then to recognise in us, a lack of straightforwardness.

Alas! They may find some of us to be both corrupt and corrupting, untruthful, power-seeking and manipulative. We are used to encountering these destructive manifestations in our own society (and, when honest, of identifying their seeds within ourselves) but I suggest that our Extra-Terrestrial brethren, who pose no threat to us whatsoever, may find that our own peculiar inner disorders constitute a potential hazard to themselves.

The nature of this principle of disorder, which in itself is external to humanity but with which Earthly mankind's own disorder all too readily resonates, is not the subject of this present study. I suggest that it is best understood as an Earth-bound condition, and the poetry of Biblical references, in both the Old and New Testaments, lends support for such a view. As such it is of relevance to that experience of exile and of separation from both God and the true self that lies at the heart of the human condition. If, as there might be some reason to suppose, we are alone among the wider humanity in living upon this dimension, wavelength or plane of being, then this sense of exile is not without substance.

The cure to our Earthly human condition is not, I suggest, a change of wavelength back to where we might have been and upon which our Extra-Terrestrial brethren seem to abide. It is rather a New Creation involving both them and ourselves.

CHAPTER FIFTEEN

THE idea of Divine Incarnation comes naturally and is, at the same time, impossible to grasp. Intervention from the very heart of The Mystery into the confused and disordered human situation is at once both highly desirable and most undesirable. It is desirable if it points a clear direction for mortal men and women to take and to follow. It is most undesirable if it then compels them to take it, willy-nilly, for the overriding of human will dehumanises the human, effectively destroying the very humanity originally bestowed upon mortal men and women.

THE AVATARA

The *Avatara* of the Hindu tradition, of whom Rama and Krishna are the obvious examples, appears on the Earthly stage in order to point the way. He is not born, nor does he die. The *Avatara* is a mythological figure, not an historical. Myth, however, is more eloquent than history, for it is poetry rather than prose and it therefore speaks to deeper levels and articulates what cannot otherwise be said.

The Buddha is also an *Avatara*-like figure. Gautama was an historical person of great holiness and inspiration but he is now exalted into mythology. In Gautama Buddha, the *Avatara* has touched ground. He has re-established, re-enlightened the *Dharma*, that word, difficult to translate, which means both the spiritual tradition and the way of life which is consequent upon it. The *Avatara* is, first and foremost, a teacher and a pointer of mortal men and women in the right direction. Krishna, in one tradition, and Buddha in another, both upheld and moved forward the *Dharma*, but what is their status?

Krishna is the *Avatara* (mythical incarnation) of Vishnu, the Creator, as understood t within the Vaishnava tradition of Hinduism. Gautama Buddha is more nearly an incarnation of the *Dharma* itself within a tradition in which all is Mind and in which all "deities" are themselves but the thoughts of Mind. Buddhism can relate to The Mystery but not, ultimately, to God.

Why do *Avataras* appear? Why are they a spiritual and mythological necessity? The answer is clear: to safeguard the *Dharma!* Their function is to point Earthly humanity in the direction of integration and fulfilment. In their own, quite different, ways, they are a response to the problems caused by "the Fall of Adam."

THE ARCHETYPAL IMAGE

The *Avatara*, incarnation or manifestation in flesh and blood of Divinity, is a deeply rooted and almost universal tradition, in some form or another. At a somewhat lower level, archetypal figures and forces are "imaged" in a broadly similar way. The mythology proclaims, in poetic fashion, the origins and self-understanding of a people. There is a central, mythic figure, a hero, who may or may not be identified with a half-forgotten historical person. The hero is a "saviour" of his people and their leader in battle. Often he is finally overcome and dies at the hands of a traitor at what is understood to be the "end of an age."

The immediate and obvious example is that of Arthur, the heroic king of Logres, the mythological undergirding of Britain. Arthur is an archetypal image but his historical prototype might have been a tribal King in South Wales, or the *Dux Bellorum* of that name, a cavalry general, who won a series of important battles against the invading Anglo-Saxons, culminating in the battle of Badon in, or near, the year AD 500. What matters about Arthur, however, is not the historical figure but the mythology, *the understanding* and *the self-understanding* that the mythology enshrines.

Here it must clearly be stated that mythology is a vehicle for the articulation and understanding of profound truths. The casual and superficial identification of the word "myth" with "lie" betrays both a distressing illiteracy and a profound ignorance.

THE ANOINTED ONE

The Hebrew word *Messiah* means "anointed one," and *Christos* is its rendering in the Greek in which the New Testament books were written. This in turn gives us the Latin *Christus* and the English *Christ*. The idea of anointing involves the Divine choice of an individual, his setting apart for the task that is given to him, and the bestowal of the authority necessary for the performance of that task. Kings and priests were anointed at the time of their entry into their specific and "set apart" responsibilities. An expectation, built up over several centuries of trial, was of the eventual coming of *the anointed one* from God, and that he would "save" his people. The Hebrew word *Israel* means "the people of God." The ideas – if not the actual institutions – of kingship and priesthood are built into that expectation.

Traced back to its Hebrew origins, the word "saviour" means "the one who helps." A saviour, therefore, is one who *establishes the conditions which make it possible for men and women to help (or save) themselves*. This might well involve teaching, and it might equally involve leadership, but first and foremost it is a matter of *being* rather than *doing*.

A saviour must first of all *be* whatever is necessary to effect the help (salvation) required. All the activity he may engage in, all his *doing*, is entirely consequent upon his *being*. The Anointed One must therefore *be in himself* whatever it is that he seeks to accomplish.

THE INCARNATION

All is Mind. All things are thoughts in the Mind of The Mystery, for God is in all things and all things are in God. The *Avatara* and the archetypal image of the mythological hero are deeply established thought-patterns both of Mind and of the myriad minds and groups of minds which partake of Mind. What we experience as physical creation is the tangible expression of ideas and intentions. The Universe, and any and all other possible Universes, are equally thought-patterns within the Mind of All.

Mind, therefore, is not devoid of imagination! Love is the entire character of The Mystery and, in the poetry of the Christian doctrine of the Holy Trinity, the unfathomable Essence of The Mystery is a Love-Affair.

The Incarnation, in the person of Jesus of Nazareth, transcends and fulfils all possible *Avataras* and archetypal images. Mythology and the decidedly tangible, flesh-and-blood, here-and-now are forever united in the one who "suffered under Pontius Pilate," that inadequate Roman official providing the specific historical reference-point. Jesus is the Ultimate Saviour for only he, in his own being, *already is in himself what he purposes to effect*.

Jesus is *the Christ*, the ultimate "anointed one," in that the two essential Natures, Divinity and humanity, Creator and created, are present and united in him. In Jesus the Christ, as one of the early Fathers of the Christian Church, boldly but faithfully, proclaimed:

God became man in order that man might become God!

The self-understanding of Earthly humanity as being in a state of exile and dis-integration makes The Incarnation seem to be, in the first instance, a specific rescue mission from the very ground of its being. Jesus of Nazareth was born of a created Mother, he grew up and lived in the context of the human condition and he suffered to the full the excesses of the paranoia and self-destruction which lie at the heart of the human condition.

In killing the humanity of The Incarnation, Earthly humanity destroyed itself. In killing God in the name of religion, pure and undefiled, the religious establishment perfectly expressed the very nature of the human condition. Nobody else could have done it! In accepting the projected self-destruction and suffering creaturely death in the humanity of Christ, the Creator bestowed a whole new potential to mankind which was revealed in the Resurrection. It is *Life on a wholly other plane of being*, Life without limitations, participation in the Eternal Life of the Creator. It is effectively the total re-creation in principle of the human race.

A Saviour is "one who helps;" who establishes the conditions whereby others can help (or save) themselves. Earthly humanity is released from identification with, and thraldom to, the principle of disorder which lies behind their condition. Individuals are invited to help (save) themselves *by consenting to believe;* by thinking it possible; by accepting in faith that which is just credible in human terms. The Divine hand is held out: Take it! The Divine Grace is always available to enable that vital step to be made, but there is no compulsion. Individual integrity – even when dis-integrated – is respected, for a faith imposed is no faith at all.

THE COSMIC IMPLICATIONS

But there is more to The Incarnation than being the specific answer to the specific ills of Earthly humanity, for the identification of Creator with creature, of God with one person – Jesus of Nazareth – of the total creature mankind, *modifies the entire creature*. The total creature can never be the same again. The implications are Cosmos-wide.

Time and time-scales, as experienced by mortal men and women, seem to have a meaning, even if the meaning cannot be clearly discerned or understood. In terms of Timelessness and of *The Eternal Now*, we are obliged to fall silent and admit defeat. Even the half-grasped understanding that time may not always be what it seems to be, nor may it always behave as we generally experience it, helps us very little. Time may run backwards and sideways for all we know, but our experience is of it running forwards, and our perceptions and understandings are limited thereby.

I suggest that we simply acknowledge that a *process* is at work, an intention is being realised, within the total creature, Mankind. Its beginning, within the context of an ultimate beginninglessness, is with The Incarnation which united both history and mythology. Its completion, within the context of endlessness, is understood as being that which, poetically, we call the *Parousia*, the Coming of Christ in Glory, the Consummation of all things. We are fumbling to articulate the promised but unimaginable and *"we know not the day nor the hour."*

I suggest that the activities of our Extra-Terrestrial brethren, who are as human as we are but different from us in their experiences of humanity, are integrally associated with this same *process* to which I have referred. If we ourselves – notwithstanding individual responses – are changed in principle by the very fact of The Incarnation, *so must they be also!*

However unconscious their motivation, their obvious fascination with Planet Earth as it and we exist on this dimension, wavelength or plane of being which is otherwise uninhabited (being uninhabitable) is, I suggest, stirred by the one underlying dynamic. We, their still disordered and long-lost brethren, were dead and are now found to be alive for evermore. We who were lost are now discovered to have been found indeed.

The lotus-throne within the mind-in-heart
reveals our human nature as its jewel,
for myth finds its embodiment in history
in man and woman both. The Word creates
the mother who shall give him birth. One flesh,
one blood; compassion at the very heart of Mystery.

PART FOUR

Daring to Guess the Unguessable.
The Quest for New Creation?

PROLOGUE TO PART FOUR

FASCINATION is a dangerous thing, obsession is more dangerous still. To identify completely with some person or some cause is to lose the ability to see him or it objectively and thus to lose the ability to make clear and responsible judgements. To become deeply involved, however, while at the same time retaining a clear detachment, is to safeguard one's own identity. It is also to be able to see issues more clearly and to attain to the possibility of that objective compassion which belongs to a mind securely set within the heart.

The Extra-Terrestrial being is, by his own nature, potentially an object to us either of disbelief and of rejection through fear, or of fascination. To become fascinated by the U.F.O. and its crew is to run the risk of becoming obsessional and fantastic. To recognise that here is a fellow human being from a very far-off land, whose inheritance of life-experience is markedly different from our own, is to reduce the risk of fascination and make a more mature response of involvement and detachment possible.

Here is a brother for whom it is appropriate to feel compassion. He is worthy of our profound respect in that he has risked his very life to find us. As he is essentially peaceful and intends us no harm whatsoever, asking of us only a brotherly greeting and acceptance, our respect for him can broaden into affection. Affection and respect are fundamental ingredients of love.

Our Extra-Terrestrial brethren come from many very different backgrounds. It is extremely difficult for us to imagine the circumstances of lives lived upon a plane of being, wavelength, dimension or what you will, which is other than our own, from which the very Universe may not look quite the same nor may it be experienced in quite the same way. Our brethren are all, however, *in this life as we are in this life;* they are not in what, to us, might seem to be an afterlife state. In dealing with them we are not dealing with a New Creation or with a state of being such as we have come to call Heaven. Nor are we dealing, let it be said, with some underworld state of animation, nor with the demonic.

I suggest that it is rather the case that our Extra-Terrestrial brethren are also in Quest for the New Creation and that it is this underlying dynamic at the very heart of things which – possibly unconsciously – brings them to where, all unexpectedly, they may actually find it.

CHAPTER SIXTEEN

MIND is the simplest and most direct metaphor we have for The Ultimate Mystery, about the essence of which we can know nothing. We may say, therefore, that all is Mind and that all created minds – themselves thoughts of the Eternal Mind – partake of Mind itself. From this we may conclude that all created minds partake of sufficient in common to allow a measure of commerce between them.

We and our Extra-Terrestrial brethren partake of the common mind of the creature, Mankind. Our different experiences, over vast tracts of time, and possibly with a different experience of space, will mean that, for both parties, there will be areas of mind which are opaque either to other. Nevertheless, communication is possible, and the telepathic communication of essential meaning translates in each communicating mind.

MIND-TO-MIND COMMUNICATION

Telepathy operates on a great many different levels. The word itself is unsatisfactory and has gathered to itself confusing and unhelpful associations. It is more satisfactory, in our present context, to speak of mind-to-mind communication. Mind-to-mind communication is always subject to subjective influences in the receiving mind and great care must be taken both to minimise this as far as possible and also – most importantly – to avoid regarding a mentally received communication as if it were a Holy Gospel!

Frequently, in mind-to-mind communication, the essential and authentic thing communicated becomes embroidered as the receiving mind over-runs the actual communication to add subjective echoes of its own. If the communication has been written down, these embroideries are not usually too difficult to detect. This subjective embroidering is particularly evident in psychic, or psycho-spiritual, communications with discarnate human souls who are concerned to impart insights and understandings to kindred spirits in Earthly life.

Mind-to-mind communication between ourselves and the Extra Terrestrial is somewhat different, however. We are both in the same "world," albeit upon different wavelengths of it. We are both human and we are both in the process of encounter with brethren of different cultures and environmental backgrounds. Our encounter is effected, in most cases, by a form of technology to which we are able to relate in principle, even if we do not yet understand its mode of operation.

As with any visitor to hitherto unvisited foreign parts, our visitors are consumed with curiosity to learn about us and – to a much lesser extent – about the world which we inhabit. Our opportunity to learn about them is somewhat more limited as we are the astonished "hosts" and they are the still wary but eagerly interested travellers whose own home environments are as yet a complete mystery to ourselves.

Mind-to-mind communication is most usually associated with psychism and that area of interest which, for want of a better word, we call occult. In order to free ourselves from this unhelpful association a simple diagram will help us. It is so simple that it may be drawn as clearly in the imagination as on paper. It is a simple cross, set upright. If we position ourselves at the intersection of the vertical and the horizontal we may discern three essential directions in which our mind-to-mind communications may proceed.

The first, diagrammatically, reaches vertically upwards. This represents to us communication with, and through, the Higher Self to the New Creation and the Source of all Being. The words "God" and "Heaven" sum it up for us and this is the realm of mind-to-mind communication on the truly spiritual, or mystical, levels at which that which is natural in us has been transfigured by the Divine Grace.

The second, again diagrammatically, reaches vertically downwards. This represents to us, not hell and the demonic (in terms of our present concerns) but rather the Inner Planes of Earth, the Earthbound post-mortem planes of being and the Elemental planes. This is the realm of the purely natural, psychic levels of communication.

Our third direction is the entire horizontal plane on a 360 degree arc. This represents to us, diagrammatically, the present-life planes of being which we share with each other, with the rest of sentient creation on Earth, and with our Extra-Terrestrial brethren. On this "horizontal" plane, mind-to-mind communication is to such a degree a commonplace that we are inclined not even to notice it. It operates – observably if we are prepared to look – upon a great many different levels. It is, for ourselves, a function of the intuitive faculty; the words "psychic" and "spiritual" carry overtones which seem inappropriate on this plane. The interpretation of intuitive perception is a function of the faculty of reason, as is also the important task of challenge and of interrogation of the intuition itself.

Our diagram must now be dismantled, for nothing is as simply categorised as we might wish it to be. If we cling, dogmatically, to our diagram and what it helps us to grasp, we shall make an idol of it, our understanding will be inhibited and we may well be led astray by our own innate capacity for being so led. Our diagram has served its purpose and now we make an end of it.

THE LINKING OF MINDS AND MIND-SYSTEMS

Mind-to-mind communication, once firmly established, can become quite articulate. Caution and great recollection are necessary, however, if subjective over-running and its subsequent embroideries are to be avoided. Mind-to-mind communication concentrates upon the immediate and the essential, for it is demanding both of considerable energy and of the profoundest recollection.

Communicating minds speak to that which is common, or sufficiently common, to both parties. There are considerable parts of the Extra-Terrestrial mind which are quite opaque to ourselves. By the same token there is a great deal within our own minds which is altogether outside the Extra-Terrestrials' experience. I suggest that our sense of identification with, and our love for, our own environment, its beauty and its creatures is something that not all Extra-Terrestrials can relate to with ease. Similarly, we may be slow to appreciate matters appertaining to their cultures and the difficulties associated with them. On their part, although as human as we are – and thus as fallible – they may be quite unprepared for the darkness, the spirit of self-destruction and the latent paranoia which lie close to the surface of the Earthly, human mind.

Once a mental link is established, through individuals who trust each other and regard each other with affection and respect, a channel is opened from mind to mind through which insights and understandings may begin to flow. As no human mind exists in isolation but partakes at unconscious levels, and in some part, of all other minds – indeed of very Mind itself – this flow of insights and understandings will spread far beyond the individuals to the whole of the human group and race, and indeed to the whole of that species within the human totality.

This is a two-way process. Our Extra-Terrestrial brethren will learn immeasurably more of us through the establishment of mental links with unfrightened individuals than ever they will by the performance of aerobatics across the wavelengths and in and out of both our visual range and the detecting capabilities of our radar systems.

There are, however, a great many different groups – even species – of Extra-Terrestrial. They vary considerably in appearance, in culture, in technology, in development and in what we might describe as maturity. I make so bold as to suggest that not all our visitors are even inhabitants of our own Universe – a very difficult thought to grasp and keep hold of – nor do all of them necessarily know of all the others' existence. I also make so bold as to suggest that none of them entertain the slightest hostile intentions towards us, nor do they constitute a threat, either to us or to our environment.

It has to be acknowledged, however, that certain groups of Extra-Terrestrial fail to manifest the extreme courtesy and respect for persons that is a characteristic, certainly of the more mature and, as a general rule, of our Extra-Terrestrial brethren as a whole. To experience this courtesy personally is, I suggest, quite a salutary lesson for us in old-fashioned good manners! To experience arbitrary and inappropriate treatment from the less mature, as if one were a zoological specimen, however well-intentioned and harmless they intend to be, can be somewhat less than pleasing. I offer a personal, light-hearted and not uncompassionate comment upon the latter:

> *I do not like a needle in the guts!*
> *I do not like a needle in the arm!*
> *I strongly disapprove – no "ifs" or "buts" –*
> *though quite persuaded that they mean no harm.*
>
> *I disapprove of needles up the nose*
> *of my dear wife, lying asleep in bed!*
> *I hope the little blighters' blood all froze*
> *and stood aghast at all the things she said!*

> *Perhaps some bug-eyed boffin in the sky*
> *has us on flying saucer's radar screen;*
> *computers up whatever she and I*
> *are doing, or records where we have been.*
>
> *"Earth-man is drinking. Whisky, I can tell;*
> *"How odd! He drank it yesterday as well!"*

SEARCHING THE MEMORIES

A common humanity presupposes a common heritage and it is tempting to search the myths, legends and sacred scriptures of the world for some clue as to what this common heritage might hold in respect of the apparent separation of Earthly mankind from their brethren who are, to us, Extra-Terrestrial.

Reference has already been made to the Adam and Eve myth and their casting out of Paradise in what could be interpreted almost as a fall from species. We must sit lightly indeed to such interpretations but it is intriguing to discover similar myths among certain of the North American Indians. Here we find a Paradisal garden, complete with a tree, although in this myth, archetypal mankind *fell through and down* into a lower world of life and being.

Chapter six of the book of Genesis contains curious references to the *Nephilim*, a "race of giants" who took wives of the children of men. The Fathers of the early Church generally identified them as fallen angels – fallen creatures of some kind, that is to say – and there may be some connection with the widespread myth of the Titans, who tried to storm heaven (i.e: become Divine on their own terms) and were cast out. The reference is puzzling, and puzzling it must probably remain, but it is not beyond the bounds of possibility that myths of this character enshrine a half-remembered calamity of truly Cosmic proportions.

By the same token, I suggest that the equally curious myths of both the Tower of Babel – in which mankind is again threatening to storm heaven, after a fashion – and Noah's Flood may retain a trace of the same corporate memory, together with other folk-memories with which they may have become amalgamated. We must be cautious, however, for we do not know and are probably unlikely ever to know. If we are wise we sit lightly to our speculations of this sort.

The myth of Atlantis is, perhaps, nearer to hand. It refers to a "lost Continent" which sank beneath the waves in cataclysmic circumstances, somewhere beyond the Straits of Gibraltar. From the apparently Mediterranean origins of this myth this indicates the unknown regions of the far-off Atlantic Ocean. The myth may enshrine more than one folk-memory of catastrophe, perhaps as does the Biblical inundation myth of Noah to which we have referred.

Speculation of many different kinds has interpreted Atlantis in glamorous guise. It sank, so it is sometimes claimed, under the weight of its own iniquity. It was an advanced civilisation, so speculation would have it, full of all manner of technological and magical wizardry, generally misapplied. Speculation indeed, but interesting in that there has been a need among such speculators so to speculate. Atlantis is a happy-hunting-ground for schools of psychism and esotericists of all kinds who have enquired of the "Inner Planes" to obtain answers to their questions, and who, I respectfully suggest, have possibly been fobbed off with Inner Plane speculations for all their pains!

The Inner Planes and their inhabitants are no more likely to be able to supply realistic answers than their eager interrogators, whatever "truths" and "teachings" they may – or may not – communicate. The reason for this is clear, if the Atlantis myth and others we have mentioned relate, however hazily and partially, to an exile to Earth upon this "wavelength" of a part of humanity from some other and original plane of being.

Why is the reason so clear? Simply that the Inner Planes themselves are unlikely to extend "further back" – to put it simplistically – than mankind's arrival upon Earth. The "Masters" or "Inner Plane Adepti," whom occultists and other psychic enthusiasts seek to consult, cannot tell us what they do not know, although some may pretend to a greater knowledge than they possess; a very human characteristic. I suggest that what Jung described as *the Collective Unconscious*, in respect of Earthly mankind, is probably contained within the same, admittedly unimaginable, parameters.

There remain to us things that we do not know, may never know, and about which we can only seek to make guesses of a variable degree of intelligence! To what folk-memories our Extra-Terrestrial brethren are inheritors we can make no guesses at all – as yet. They are quite inaccessible to us – as yet. The present moment and its demands are quite sufficient to command our attentions. Any mind-to-mind communication that may take place with Extra-Terrestrials is likely to be of a very immediate character for a very long time.

CHAPTER SEVENTEEN

THE Earthly, human mind, being what it is, has a tendency to draw back from the unexpected and to retreat behind the comfortingly familiar. The more uncomfortable perceptions of the intuitive faculty are therefore rationalised out of the way and a sense of ease and comfort is thus restored. A rationalistic society prefers to live in a world of two dimensions only; with *area* it is comfortable, but *volume* terrifies!

The sophisticated rationalist will tend to interpret any perceptions out of the ordinary in terms of sickness. If the message is too disturbing then it is a simple matter to decide that the messenger is psychologically disturbed. One can then go back to bed! The human condition tends to demand: "Don't do anything different, don't think anything which everybody else is not thinking, don't see, hear or perceive anything which is at all out of the ordinary. In short, don't rock the intellectual boat!"

A study such as the one upon which we are engaged cannot be other than "politically incorrect" to the highest degree. Anybody with half a mind or none can drive a coach and horses through its every argument with the greatest of ease. *There are, however, no arguments presented. All is suggestion only, for it can be none other.* No man or woman who has not experienced can assess or interpret with any certainty another man's or woman's experience. Even the useful science of psychology is limited by the psychology of the psychologist, his or her hidden fears, preconceptions and subjective motivations. Only God is God!

The question must be asked: "Is what has here been suggested at all credible?" The answers arrived at will depend upon those answering, and in particular their ability *to think without fear*. In the last resort, however, this pudding, like any other, finds its proof in the eating. There is no other way.

In the meantime, therefore, there is nothing for it but to go on, thinking laterally across the sacred boundaries of religion, science and the occult. The risk must be run of causing outrage to religionists, irritation to scientists and antagonism in occultists, inviting ridicule and denunciation from all points of the compass. But this is a task which only a fool would – or could – attempt and the writer, from the very first page, lays claim to no other status whatsoever!

GROWTH TOWARDS AN END-PRODUCT

Everything in the whole of creation, every creature according to its order and in its own way, has its beginning, its growth and development, and its fulfilment or fruition. After all these there is an end and a new beginning. This is observably the case for everything that Earthly man experiences and is capable of observing. Similarly, a train of thought, conceived and set in motion, follows through to its own conclusions and fulfilment, thus generating another new beginning or set of beginnings. Each newly generated thought, or creation, begins its own journey towards a new stage of new-beginning-generating fulfilment.

Mind is our metaphor for *The Mystery* whose essence is unfathomable. All is mind, and our created minds are thoughts of, and partakers in, Mind itself. "God is in all things, all things are in God." This is another way of saying the same thing in different terms.

We ourselves are conceived and born into this world. We grow to maturity, towards fruition, and then we die into a new beginning. What we may describe as the universal "old religion" of Earthly man seems to have interpreted this in terms of re-birth into this same world, life succeeding life, thus making any Earthly life-span part of a larger and longer process of becoming, with a greatly extended journey towards maturity and fruition. The developed World Religions of Hinduism and Buddhism firmly enshrine this once probably universal belief.

I suggest that this belief is inherited, if not built-in, to mankind. I suggest that it may represent the memory of a pre-fallen self-understanding which operates universally in an undisturbed natural order. In terms of our Earthly condition, however, it fails to deliver its intended fulfilment, for in us the old Natural order is dis-ordered. I suggest that it may belong to human life as still lived, and far more widely, upon another wavelength, dimension or plane of being. It cannot succeed upon this one because, in the language of Biblical mythology, Adam and Eve have thrown in their lot with the serpent and are cast out.

The re-birth mechanism, for us once total-humanity-wide and leading naturally towards an end product, is now only Earthly-humanity-wide and is contained within a drastically limited state of Earth-boundness. The hope, in this dispensation, is for eventual release from *Samsara;* release, that is to say, from a Cosmic jail-situation. We can only speculate as to the fulfilment understandings of our Extra-Terrestrial brethren. Indeed, to such an extent may it be an essentially unruffled natural process that – unlike us – they may not devote a great deal of time or energy to thinking about it!

ENLARGING OUR VISION OF THINGS

Until now we have interpreted everything pertaining to mankind only in terms of Earth and the human condition of mortal men and women. The religious quest is, I suggest, a peculiarly Earthly phenomenon in that it is *a quest*, a search for lost meaning and integrity and an urgent pressing forward towards a future, be it Earthly or Heavenly, which has got to be, for us, better than the past or the present.

The Incarnation has been interpreted by Christian Believers only in terms of Earthly human sinfulness and bondage, and the release from both into a New Humanity and the life of Grace which it took place precisely in order to effect. The promise of the *Parousia*, the coming again of the Son of Man in glory, has been at once a central hope and a puzzle. The puzzle has tended to push the hope out of sight under a growing pile of very human religious institutions.

The Incarnation began *a process* among Earthly men and women which has yet to be completed. It is a process which involves both Earthly life and the life beyond, with the New Humanity transcending the boundaries between the two. Heaven, a state of being, a new integrity, a new contract for human existence and a new relationship both with and within *The Mystery* begins, for those who will, in the context of their Earthly lives.

We now face a new and hitherto unimagined challenge. Here are *other human beings*, both different to ourselves and at the same time essentially the same as ourselves, tentatively visiting us from wholly other realms, *yet in this same mortal life*. The Incarnation is for them as well as for us, but probably in a different way and perhaps for different reasons.

I suggest that our Extra-Terrestrial brethren are, like ourselves, on the threshold of whatever is meant by the *Parousia*. It may be that, in them, the human creation has come to a fruition in the old natural order and that they are close to the end of their possibilities. It may be that human life on Earth is also close to the end of its possibilities of fruition. I suggest that the Incarnation, so far from being an essentially religious concern, is in fact the New Beginning, the New Heaven and the New Earth, already present and operative within the totality of humanity, in advance of whatever endings may, or may not, transpire.

All this is speculation but I suggest that it is a necessary and responsible exercise so long as the temptation to write scenarios is most firmly resisted. As the Incarnate Lord said, of his coming again:

> "Stay awake, because you do not know either the day or the hour."
> *(Matt 25: 13)*

Our responsibilities are firmly fixed in the present moment and grand exercises in detailed speculation, backwards or forwards in time, can be practically guaranteed to "take the eye off the ball" and wonderfully inflate the individual's ego in the process.

The New Testament does require, however, that Christian Believers expect and ever look towards a consummation, a fulfilment. The necessarily poetic descriptions that are sometimes given suggest an occurrence of truly Cosmic proportions. It is a New Heaven and a New Earth that are in the making after all! I suggest that it is better, in any event, to think big and expect bigger rather than to shrink back into a thinking which becomes smaller and ever smaller, and which ultimately reduces the Escatological Hope to a dry, two-dimensional academic rationalisation.

CHAPTER EIGHTEEN

KEEPING OUR HEADS ABOVE THE WATER

A CENTRAL concept in Buddhist mysticism is "The voidness of the non-void." Put in slightly different terms it is the ultimate no-thing-ness of things. It is a reminder that no creature has any ultimate existence in its own right. All are expressions of an intention hid unfathomably within the very heart of The Mystery. A wise man once suggested that creatures exist, in the first instance, as archetypal sets of proportions within the mind of God and, as St John reminds us:

"God is love." (1 Jn 4: 16)

The Mystery is No-Thing but, as we have just been reminded, *The Mystery is Love*. Love gives thing-ness to things for Love's sake and for the love of the things themselves in all the possibilities of their thing-ness. Mind – let it be suggested again – is our best metaphor for The Mystery and it is the imagination of the Mind of Love which bestows upon us our image-hood, our thing-ness. So behold! Things *are*, and we exist!

It is very necessary that, from time to time, we remind ourselves of the ultimate no-thing-ness of things, the status of the entire Universe and of all other possible Universes as figments of the loving imagination of the Mind of Love. Why? Because we are buried up to our ears in thing-ness all day long. It is fatally easy to miss the wood of No-Thing for all the multitude of trees of thing-ness! In our present study this error is, I suggest, of all things to be avoided.

Being ourselves "things," our lives are lived in the context of thing-ness. I cut my finger and I bleed. All philosophy vanishes at the first sign of toothache. As one Chinese scholar once put it, "I prefer pork to poetry!" My small, semi-detached house is a magician's cave of science and technology at their every level. The very red bricks of which it is built are proof of that, at one level; the medicines in the bathroom cupboard and the word-processing programme on my computer are further proofs at different, and more profound, and even bewildering, levels.

Things in their thing-ness abound and hedge me in upon every side. I look up into the sky and I know that, beyond the clouds, space-probes are, at this moment, on their way to, or on their way from, other planets in the solar system. The behaviour of all these various bodies is known to a degree of accuracy which enables things to be calculated and communicated through other things, to yet other things, in order to achieve pin-point accuracy in terms of orbitally moving objects at unimaginable speeds and at Cosmic distances. Things in their thing-ness reign supreme.

The Incarnation represents *the Deification of things and the thing-ness of things;* it is a ringing endorsement of the non-void from the very heart of the Void. If we will, it enables us to attain to an equilibrium which can take poly-dimensional paradox in its stride.

Our difficulty, particularly in what we think of as "Western Civilisation," is that we are prisoners of our own logic and logic is two-dimensional, if not positively linear. The more clever we become, the less we see around us. Perhaps, therefore, it is not surprising that many, who are held in the remorseless mindsets that scientific research demands, find their release into a greater sense of wholeness in quite surprisingly simplistic forms of religious faith and devotion.

Science and technology, as we know and experience them, represent the triumph of rationality and rational invention. They are children of the Renaissance when science parted company, both with the stultifying influence of a corrupted and all-powerful religious institution which sought to regulate and control all human thought, and also with its own intuitive framework of understanding and insightful speculation. From this separation emerged three arguably unbalanced disciplines; the physical sciences, shorn of their own "soul"; the intuitive sciences, driven into an "occult" corner – and institutionalised religion as a thing on its own, having largely parted company with life! This disruption has been, in very many ways, quite calamitous, and the responsibility for it can be fairly and squarely laid at the door of the religionist.

It is now time for a new lateral thinking to take place within these three disciplines, not only to effect necessary repairs to all three, but to move towards a new wholeness altogether. In such a climate, the thing-ness of things and *the within* of things will re-focus in the mind of the observer. In such a climate, the non-absoluteness of what we see, measure and manipulate from that dimension, wavelength, plane of being (or what you will) upon which we currently stand will also become increasingly clear.

A TERMINOLOGICAL QUEST

The term "Inner Space" is sometimes used for the infinitesimal universe which is revealed in atomic and sub-atomic research. After all, one looks "outer" through a telescope and "inner" through a microscope, so the application of such terminology has a certain logic about it. I suggest that the term is better used, however, to describe *the within of things,* the inner, "psychic" realities of which the physical are the expressions or manifestations.

To a very limited degree, the disciplines of occultism have to do with what might be described as the psychic nuts and bolts of things, and also with the possibilities of transcending time and space limitations within necessarily Earthbound parameters. That such studies are open to misapplication by fallible men and women is obvious, but as much can be said for the externals, as the rape of the environment and the commercial squandering of finite resources testify. We are not concerned, in this study, with the passing of judgements, or with fear.

The activities of the occultist are limited. Considerable insights are to be gained as to the working of things, the dynamics of Creation as we encounter them, and of the counterbalancing forces that influence ourselves and our lives. There is a strong magico-mystical element in certain forms of occultism which constitutes, in part at least, a profound religious quest. The discipline is, however, essentially Earthbound. Nature must be transformed and transfigured by Grace before the magical can become the truly mystical.

The brief glimpses that may be given into, and across, the Inner Space are indeed "given" and not sought, and they are of an essentially mystical character. Inner space contains the Outer and all its "things." It is fatally easy, when using these terms, to fall into the two-dimensional tidy-mindedness of the "civilised Westerner" and to claim that "therefore, *this* is the same as *that,* and *that* is merely another term to describe *the other*." Inner Space is not what Buddhists mean by *The Void,* nor is it simply to be equated with Mind Itself for it has, fundamentally, to do with the thing-ness of things.

I suggest that Inner Space has to do – among other things – with *the mechanics of possibility*, and this must surely include the apparent wavelength or dimension-changing activities of our Extra-Terrestrial brethren. Inner Space is also, I suggest, *a medium of communication*. It might almost be described as "the organising field of Creation," but that might suggest a human capacity to understand, to pin-down, to make tidy and to control. It is better that Inner Space remain, for us, the profound and silencing mystery that it is.

THE SOUND OF ONE HAND, CLAPPING
In the last resort, the problems arising from the mind's acceptance of the Extra-Terrestrial as a reality, and not merely as an indication of someone else's psychological disturbance, must resemble those connected with the Zen Buddhist's "Sound of one hand, clapping." Our normal categories of thought and everyday experience are overcome and have to be re-negotiated, even transcended.

We ourselves are deeply mired in thing-ness and its apparently immutable rules, both of behaviour and of existence. We are further inhibited by the deeply pervasive rationalism of our Western culture and its innate tendency to pay a quite undue reverence to logic. All things have their rightful place and so, most decidedly, does logic, but there are higher logics than our own.

"The sound of one hand, clapping," pitchforks us, if we will allow it, into a new and far wider field of perceptions.

CHAPTER NINETEEN

A MANNER OF SEEING AND NOT SEEING

I SUGGEST that there may be good reason to suppose that, although the majority of our Extra-Terrestrial brethren are usually invisible to our normal vision (though sometimes visible, to varying degrees, to the inner eye), we are nevertheless visible to their own form of vision. In addition I believe it may be true to say that at least the more developed and mature Extra-Terrestrials see not only the person *but also that person's aura*, and are thus able to discern something at least of the character of the person with whom they are seeking to relate.

I suggest that it may well be the case that hierarchy, among the more mature groups at least, is determined by that which is revealed in the aura and thus visible to all. This is very far indeed from the case among mortal men and women whose sensitivities seldom extend to clairvoyant vision of another's aura, though this is a well known capacity in the comparatively few. Human life on Earth might take on a somewhat different character if auras, and what they reveal, were visible to all!

This probable difference in discernment capability has two important effects. The first is the perplexity experienced by some at least of our Extra-Terrestrial visitors as to why our society is ordered the way it is. The second is, perhaps fortunately, an ability in them to discern the character, and thus the possible motives, of those who may be at pains to initiate communications with them.

Official denials and disinformation in respect of all manner of things, besides the Extra-Terrestrial, are a commonplace and are decreasingly credible. The always slightly tattered cloak of official secrecy suggests that somewhere, somebody is likely to be attempting contact with Extra-Terrestrials on an official, or demi-official level. Obsessions with national security and the possible military application of revolutionary technology will be compounded with the urgent manipulations of the obsessionally power-hungry in anything of the sort that may be going on. It is as well that character discernment may be a capability built in to our brethren although essentially lost among ourselves.

I suggest that there is reason to suppose that the aura of Earth, on this "wavelength," has that about it which is extremely disturbing and disruptive of the mind-machine technology which is very probably a feature of Extra-Terrestrial vehicles. It is upsetting of the mental equilibrium necessary for the control of both their reconnaissance vehicles and their larger craft. I suggest that this is that self-same disturbance which is both the root-cause of our present alienation and which is that from which the Incarnation has delivered us into the way of re-creation.

Our Extra-Terrestrial brethren are human and evolve, like ourselves and all other sentient creatures, by processes of trial and error. They are far from perfect and they are also far from being infallible. They make mistakes and they are capable of foolishness, just like us. But I suggest that they are not, like us, afflicted by and partially identified with a spirit of alienation, self-destruction and paranoia . Their encounter with this, both in us and in Earth's aura, is a matter of considerable perplexity and disturbance to them and might be sufficient to repel them from us altogether. There is, however, a profound, underlying and unconscious dynamic which brings them here and which causes them to keep on coming, despite all perplexities and hazards.

PARADOX AND PERPLEXITY

The Christian understanding of the dis-order and dis-integration of human life on Earth is that it has ever been such as to require healing by re-creation only. It is not possible for us to delve into pre-history in search of an age of innocence, however tempting the exercise might seem, nor is it possible to speculate meaningfully as to the mechanics of the unfathomable. We can only begin from where we are, and from our own experience, such as we understand it.

The Christian Religion – *as opposed to the Christian Revelation* – is but one among a number of major World Religions. The Incarnation did not take place in order to found a new and better religion, nor was it concerned to reform an existing one. The Incarnation transcends all these categories altogether for it was not a "religious" initiative from the very heart of The Mystery. God is not "religious" and the poetry of the New Testament reminds us that there is no Temple in the Heavenly Jerusalem.

In the Christian understanding, the Incarnation took place not to repair damage or even – as in the case of the *Avatara* – to uphold and secure the *Dharma*. Its purpose was the re-creation of the Creature, Mankind, from within. Love knows only "all or nothing," and Earthly Mankind had to be suffered, and henceforth suffered hereafter, to be itself participator in the work of its own re-creation, for individual free-will commands an absolute respect from Love. The Individual is given every assistance by the Divine Grace to actively participate in the work of its own New Becoming but the road is exceedingly rocky and demands all or nothing from the depths of the individual's being.

It would be arrogant, and indeed absurd, to suppose that the Life of Grace is only open to those institutionalised into observant Christian religionism. The Church, in the eyes of Heaven, is unimaginably bigger, wider and more diverse than the ranks of the formally confessing, baptised and attending Churchpeople of whatever denomination. God is the only judge and knows the hearts and fundamental desires of every man and woman, of whatever race, colour or creed.

There is, therefore, both an aura and a corporate Mind which is of the order of Nature transfigured into re-creation by Grace. *The Mind of Christ is the corporate Mind of those in the Way of re-creation* and it transcends the boundaries of mortal earthly, and post-mortem Heavenly life. It is this with which the Extra-Terrestrial is coming into contact *as well as* the disturbed mind and polluted aura of Earth and Earthly humanity. The Extra-Terrestrial is thus encountering a process in operation, not only at the depths of the being of Earthly humanity as he is beginning to encounter it, *but at the depths of his own being as well.* His problems in coming to terms with it, and its implications, are not quite the same as ours but they are no less perplexing.

I suggest that it is probable that religion, as we know it and experience it, is unlikely to be found among our Extra-Terrestrial brethren. Religion is the product of our circumstances, not theirs. I suggest that Order, and Law, are the bases upon which their societies function and that forgiveness for transgression may have a somewhat different meaning and application for them.

We know none of these things. We can only speculate and make suggestions, but there may be reason to suppose that the more mature of our Extra-Terrestrial brethren are already somewhat exercised by the perplexities of a paradox for which they were completely unprepared.

The appearance of Extra-Terrestrials and their vehicles in our Earthly airspace has been, and remains, a cause of perplexity which invites a number of very human responses from us. The first, that of unacknowledged fear, is an arrogant and contemptuous dismissal of the whole thing as nonsense and the product of the psychological problems of other people. This may be expressed in a number of different professional "jargons" but it is still the response of fear.

The second response is equally unsatisfactory. It is represented by uncritical acceptance, fascination and even obsession with the whole subject. Cults of the U.F.O. and the E.T. spring up, both quasi-religious and quasi-scientific, and objectivity flies out of the window.

The third, more sinister, response – also prompted largely by fear – is the determination to use for power whatever may be found usable in this situation. Power, in this connection, may be occult, political or military or – nastiest of all – a combination of all three.

It is a matter of some difficulty to keep the head clear and the feet on the ground in the face of apparent visitation by persons hitherto unknown and unimagined and – apparently – from a completely different dimension, wavelength or plane of being. There does not yet exist a terminology that can express even this! If this phenomenon is as objective as it seems to be – in a word, if it is true – then this is something of the profoundest significance, even if we have not the slightest idea what that significance might be.

A wise man once commented that science and religion are mutually opposed, but in the same way that finger and thumb are opposed. To grasp something, the two must work together. I have introduced what might seem to be a third member, namely the occult, but this is essentially the child of that unhealthy divorce between disciplines which was the fruit of the Renaissance and its rebellion against the mind-clamping tyranny of the Mediaeval Papacy. Science, religion and the occult have been isolated each in its own light-tight box and we have had a deal of poking, but altogether too little grasping, as a result.

There is very little that is occult left in occultism. The light of day has been breaking in on all sides. What remains "hidden" is fast dispersing to left and to right, into the realms of science upon the one hand, and of unfearful and laterally thinking religion on the other. Its rightful place is, arguably, as that flexible joint which enables the finger and thumb to work together, providing a measure of common ground between them and some useful terms of reference.

This study is an invitation to lateral thinking by any and all who are prepared *to think without fear*. It contains suggestions and speculations only. Were it an attempt at any kind of assertion or dogmatism it could not have included poetry in its pages, for poetry and dogmatism have nothing in common, nothing whatsoever. It is also a response to personal experience and to the challenge of that experience. It was provoked by an encounter, and the discovery within that encounter of a deep, mutual exchange of affection and respect which took the author completely by surprise.

Mutual affection and mutual respect are, perhaps, the two principle ingredients of Compassion or, if you prefer another word for it, Love.

CHAPTER TWENTY

POSTSCRIPT

THE author, in so far as he is aware, has never, so far, seen a "flying saucer" or any kind of "Unidentified Flying Object." He has never had the experience, reported by some, of having been abducted by Aliens. He has never subscribed to, and can never remember reading, a magazine or other periodical devoted to this subject.

The author has never experienced difficulties, however, in accepting the possibility of Extra-Terrestrial visitation, nor has he ever found that possibility alarming. His own interest has been stimulated by a growing realisation, over a period of perhaps five years and certainly three, that he and other members of his household have been on the "visiting list" of certain groups of "other than terrestrial persons" who have made their presences apparent, with some degree of insistence, until noticed and accepted for what, and who, they are.

Descriptions of personal experiences are open to intrusive misinterpretation by both the sceptic and the credulous. Let the matter be rather stated thus:

Unseen, half-seen;
dimensions other than the milkman and the post,
nor heaven, nor hell,
nor inner planes of mother earth –
adepti, peddlers of occult lore –
quite other.

And other, sometimes, than each other.
Some tall and shrouded, slow,
as of another Universe, and shy,
yet yielding to affection.
They come and go
and hang about their favourite place,
and one will sometimes follow on;
an unseen brother.

> *Others will come with outstretched arms*
> *and clasp my outstretched hands.*
> *The Love which has created us*
> *flows each to each;*
> *there is a meeting of quite different minds,*
> *yet not minds other.*

The Apostle Paul, in quite another context, speaks of "walking by faith and not by sight." Where normal vision is not involved – as a rule – and only the fleeting glimpses of the inner eye in what is sometimes called Clairvoyance, everything has to be taken on trust. The inner senses, psychic or psycho-spiritual, must always be interrogated until they can be trusted. Discernment, and that inner certainty of knowing *who* and *what*, are gifts which are given and are not to be lightly assumed. Nothing is available for testing under laboratory conditions any more than any normal, earthly encounter between persons can be so "tested." All has, perforce, to be taken upon trust, after which, having "walked by faith," sight – and even touch – may follow:

> *I am as one deprived of sight*
> *and made to live by trust alone.*
> *I judge not by appearances*
> *but touch the heart*
> *and, in that touching, know.*
>
> *I am as one both old and frail,*
> *supported by a gentle Word*
> *to introduce me to that heart*
> *my heart has touched;*
> *to tell me whom I know.*
>
> *Thus introduced, I open wide;*
> *love speaks to love,*
> *and all within the Love*
> *which has created both of us*
> *to love, and thus to know.*

There are, as has already been suggested, several different types, groups – even species – of Extra-Terrestrial visitor. For the most part they are characterised by a notable courtesy. They are "visiting" and they conduct themselves as well-mannered visitors. There are others, however, who seem less mature and I suggest, somewhat more humanoid than human. There may be reason to suppose that they are servants of more human masters and that they may not be, in every respect, happy at their work.

The author has not been abducted (these, I suggest, are the usual abductors if abductions indeed take place) but he has found himself to be on their "visiting list" on a number of occasions, apparently regarded by them as an interesting zoological specimen! Importunate they may have been, but the author is quite unable to feel towards them anything other than a great compassion.

Crammed full of curiosity they came;
small, self-important and grotesque,
seeing us as specimens,
prime fodder for their theses
to probe, investigate and track;
dosing our medicine to our very own selves,
yet not unkindly.

They would march in in line-ahead
to be confronted, questioned, blessed.
Or they would gather silently, at night;
and once with needle, once with probe,
brought both of us most violently awake,
their tracking implant planting,
and scattered blindly.

They came and stood before my chair,
attended to my admonitions
and faded from before my face.
Their needle-mark is fading from my arm
and they have not returned.
They held a mirror to my human pride:
I thank them kindly!

On more than one occasion of being unexpectedly visited, by the more mature of our visitors, the author has been politely invited, "Would you like to come with us?" The invitation seems to be something like a conventional courtesy. The answer given has always been. "Thank you very much, but it would not be appropriate." This seems to satisfy as being the correct answer to give!

It is the right answer – even if the opposite were a genuine option – for we are identified with our own Earthly environment in a way which may be unique. All men and women enrich each other by truly being themselves as natives of their own lands, and each giving articulation to what, in German, is called the *Heimat*. Earthly men and women have a priesthood, in many directions, and a priest is one who stands at the intersection of two worlds and is the one through whom their commerce flows. Let the matter of this book be finally stated thus:

> *I am the gateway to a wayside inn,*
> *through me the commerce flows;*
> *traces of tidings, scraps of news,*
> *all come piecemeal to multiply my peace;*
> *I take all travellers to my heart*
> *but must not cling, must wish God-speed*
> *and here most faithfully abide.*
>
> *I stand, deep-rooted into Mother Earth;*
> *through me the to-and-fro of travellers pass*
> *to pass beyond my sight*
> *along the spreading highways of that Mind*
> *that thinks us, calls us forth*
> *to be, be rooted, and to roam;*
> *both washed and carried by the tide.*
>
> *I take the travellers into my heart,*
> *see to their needs and know their ways,*
> *set thus until what end of days.*
> *The tides are turning,*
> *flowing fast;*

the time for Time is nearly past
for, Timeless, all shall soon abide.

◆

APPENDIX A

THE LIBERATION OF THE IMAGINATION

AN ESSAY

PART ONE

CONCERNING THE IMAGINATION

As a man imagines things, so are they. Everything that exists is what it is imagined to be, for the imagination, rightly understood, is objective before ever it is subjective. The imagination enables men and women to see what is, to perceive and to interpret. To a very large degree the parameters of mortal, earthly life are set by the conditioned imagination of the group. Thereafter, imagination, being stifled by its conditioning, is confined to the subjective, and both lateral thinking and lateral imagining are inhibited to a substantial degree.

All creative work involves the imagination. To break out of conventional moulds is to shock, to startle, to offend. But the artist must paint what he sees and the composer must write down what he hears. What he sees and what he hears will be dependent upon the conditionings which impose rules about how one ought to see, how one ought to hear. Lateral seeing, lateral hearing, being strange and unexpected, will often lack the disciplines of interpretation. The subjective will dominate, but it will have been a glimpse of objective vision that will have inspired the artist in whatever medium. He or she will have to find means of interpreting whole new dimensions within the dimensional parameters of mortal, earthly life.

The very Cosmos is, to a large extent, the creation of mortal man's imagination. That is to say that the conditioning of the group mind is such as to limit the perceptions of men and women to what they perceive the physical, external realities to be. Thus a number of planets, of which Earth is one, orbit the Sun and the Sun itself is a star in a galaxy, and galaxies abide in an unimaginable void called Outer Space. Mathematics and computer technology enable satellites to be sent into orbit round the Earth, landings to be made on the Moon and camera-carrying probes to be sent to far-flung planets in the solar system. All this confines the conditional parameters of mortal men and women and tramlines their imagination, leading it in the straightest of lines to an ultimate meaninglessness. The Great Question, looming unanswerable at the end of the tramline is – "So what?"

The imagination is conditioned to be unable to imagine. There are strict boundaries beyond which it is improper for the imagination to stray. The world of Science Fiction is, and must remain, fictional. Its creations are, to a large extent, but projections of the disordered psyche of mortal men, and wars and conflicts are projected into the intergalactic abyss as if the entire Cosmos were but an extension of the self-hatred and self-destructive tendencies of sinful men and women. The imagination is hard pressed to leap over these prison walls into the fresh air and wide open spaces of Reality.

The conditioned imagination cannot fit certain commonly perceived phenomena into its scheme of things. Thus the entire psychic realm, poly-dimensional and multi-layered as it is encountered by multitudes of men and women, must perforce be denied, discounted, explained away using the jargon of psychology or – even worse – arbitrarily demonised by those whose world-view, religious or secular, is threatened by the very idea of it. For this reason, in the rationalistic cultures and also in the rationalistic religious cultures which are found therein, the entire intuitive faculty is suspect. It is, for some, the realm of "the devil and his angels," in spite of the consequence of such a stance amounting to a fifty-per-cent denial of the Incarnation!

Perceived phenomena must, however, belong somewhere. There must be a time-space continuum of sorts – probably several – which is not discoverable either through the telescope of the astronomer or the microscope of the biologist. Perceived realities of an other-than-normal order may not simply be denied. To do so, a common enough response it has to be said, is simply dishonest. At best it is an ostrich reaction; a burying of heads in the sand in the hope that the embarrassment will go away. In any event such a response is pathological, even schizophrenic.

An honest acceptance of commonly perceived phenomena demands an acknowledgement that there is more to the Cosmos than the telescope reveals. Other forces are at work, other time-space continua obtain, other dimensions and levels of being abound.

It also involves the honest recognition that it is not awareness of other levels, or "inner worlds" that is pathological but the denial of the reality of any such awareness on *a priori* grounds.

The imagination is not a mechanism for dreaming up the unreal; it is the blessed faculty whereby the entire Cosmos is able to be present in the mind of Mankind as a whole, and in the individual minds of men and women as their growth in Grace and release from preconditioning determines. The imagination, being itself created, cannot go beyond the bounds of the possible in Creation. In a perverted human mind, the imagination can dwell upon the perverse with lamentable results, but all that the imagination constructs, its every image, is to some extent inherently possible in some way or another. The release of an individual's imagination from its conditioning is a blessed release indeed, although it may be some time before the products of such an imagination are open to a balanced interpretation.

The perceived phenomena which, broadly speaking, belong to the psychic realm, demand some kind of frame of reference, however conditional it might be. A working hypothesis needs to be arrived at, but such are the pressures to the contrary, from morbid fascination on the one hand to stern prohibition on religious grounds upon the other, that it is easier to allow the problems posed to remain unresolved. This is a reaction, however, not in faith in any sense whatsoever, but of fear. The construction of such working hypotheses is thus left to enthusiasts and limited interest groups and a general loss of balance is only to be expected in such constructions as are produced.

If earth-bound or earth-related phenomena, which are other than the everyday, provoke such an ostrich-like reaction, how much more must those which seem to originate elsewhere than Earth succeed in driving heads ever more deeply into the sand? For too long, and for too many people, phenomena of an apparently Extra-Terrestrial origin have been a consciously perceived reality and it is simply perverse to pretend otherwise. But what is the frame of reference which enables experiences of this sort to make sense?

The common enough assumptions that personal intelligences encountered – sometimes quite clearly, even vividly – must come from the Moon, from Mars or from Venus, have been exploded by post-war technology. The possibility that such Extra-Terrestrial visitants might be of more than one type or species adds yet another dimension to the unsolved, and so far unattempted problem.

It would not be too difficult for a cartoonist to illustrate our difficulties by drawing a line-up of ostriches, all facing the horizon but with their heads buried in the sand. Upon the rump of each might be pinned a card bearing such legends as: Scientist. Religionist. Psychologist. Sociologist and so on, every one fearful for his very own, tight little world-view and terrified of what might be revealed by the light of dawn.

It is, I suggest, the cartoonist and the poet who are best equipped to attempt the articulation of that which lies beyond the normal bounds of rationally interpreted experience. It is far from being the case that there must be a descent into irrationality; that is a sub-human reaction and to be abhorred. Rather, the reason must learn some new tricks in order to expand to the task of interpreting and interrogating an intuition whose own parameters have been widened. The cartoonist is, after all, a poet whose pencil makes pictures rather than words.

The mortal sin of rationalism is that it cannot accept Myth and Poetry for what they are. The all-too-common equation of "Myth" with "Lie" comes close to that sin against the Holy Spirit against which the Gospel warns in uncompromising terms. The hammering flat of poetry, as if upon an anvil, and the figurative nailing down of the resulting wreckage as if it had really been prose all along, is crass to the point of sub-humanity. Mortal sin is, after all, a wilful abandonment of human dignity in any event.

The imagination must be set free in faith, by faith and as an act of faith. It will construct nothing that is not, in some way, possible, for that would itself be an impossibility. The faithful offering up of its images and constructs to Truth, and to Perfect Love, will rid them of the worst of their subjective content and enable them to become vehicles for the expression of truthfulness; means whereby compassion, affection and respect may reach across boundaries hitherto unknown, to worlds and their inhabitants hitherto unimagined and unimaginable.

Yet all things abide, and shall forever abide, within the same embrace of Everlasting Love, as thoughts within the Mind of The Mystery which forever imagines us all.

IMAGINE, IF YOU CAN

Imagine, if you can, a pattern of interweaving spheres, all set within a sphere which is itself interwoven with others.

Imagine, if you can, each sphere belonging to that pattern of interwoven spheres being of infinite extent, in that it exists upon a limitless possibility of wavelengths, frequencies or such other metaphors as might suggest such a possibility.

Imagine, if you can, a narrow band of wavelengths belonging to one such sphere. (We shall use this metaphor, clearly understanding that it is but a metaphor relating to a Mystery beyond our comprehension.) Upon each wavelength, the perceptions of a thinking, rational observer will be limited to realities as they exist upon that wavelength only. The "laws of nature", of physics, of mathematics which appear to govern the functions of creatures existing upon that wavelength will be consistent with that overall consistency which governs all things. These "laws" are not, however, as absolute as they might seem to be.

This narrow band of wavelengths admits of a certain degree of interpenetration; indeed it is entirely normal for creatures essentially belonging to one to have access to others, even to exist upon more than one such wavelength at a time. A disorder at the heart of a creature will, however, inhibit both perception and normal commerce between wavelengths. That creature will tend to be imprisoned upon one band only. This is a pathological condition.

It is the lot of mortal man to be so imprisoned. For this reason he cannot perceive reality as it is, but only that wavelength upon which he abides. He can neither alter his wavelength nor readily imagine such a proceeding. His attempts to do so have, in the main, tended to imprison him the more tightly in that their underlying motivation has itself been pathological. The seeking of power or advantage by manipulative magic is, in the last resort, absolutely counter-productive.

Imagine, if you can, a wholly different dimension to each sphere, transcending all its myriad wavelengths and uniting them in relation to itself.

Imagine, if you can, a guiding intelligence at the heart of each sphere, whose character is the underlying character of every wavelength and all its creatures.

Imagine, if you can, the whole pattern of interweaving spheres, all within a sphere which is itself interwoven with others.

Imagine, if you can, an infinite progression of what has so far been suggested, all a pattern of patterns *ad infinitum*, of creative intelligences, each at the heart of a world-within-worlds of unlimited possibilities, with an infinite number of creatures, every one unique and all abiding in an all-pervading ambience of Love.

All this is but a metaphor; the reality, to which the metaphor is faithful, is of an infinitely greater glory, complexity and simplicity and is altogether beyond the capacity of a created imagination. It is, however, the very stuff of the Uncreated Imagination, within which, within whom, everything that exists is a thought, an expression, a very child of Love itself.

Imagine, if you can, within the pattern of interwoven spheres within a sphere, a certain identity of wavelengths between them. Remember that we are talking in metaphors.

Imagine if you can, human or humanoid beings existing, in slightly differing forms, on several – perhaps all – of the interwoven spheres, endowed with that natural faculty of living upon more than one wavelength at once – save for mortal man on Earth, whose condition is disordered and some of whose faculties are inhibited thereby.

Imagine, if you can, a dynamic at the very heart of things which causes humanoids from other spheres to seek to establish contact with their brother humanoids on Earth and to discover what it is that has silenced them and changed them.

Imagine, if you can, humanoids at somewhat different levels of evolution upon different spheres, stirred by the same dynamic. They will react in ways appropriate to their stages of development. Some will cross from a sphere interwoven with Earth in ways suggestive of Earthly technology. They will transfer from one sky to another, as if in flight. Their vehicles will appear and disappear to Earthly vision and apparatus. Not infrequently they will land, or come very close to landing. They will wish to investigate Earthly men, women and children but without the least intention of doing them harm, for the whole idea of deliberately inflicting pain or damage is quite foreign to them.

Others will cross the bounds without recourse to technology. They will be among the more highly developed and will be characterised by their evident respect for their Earthly counterparts and their great courtesy towards them. All will respond to affection and a welcoming heart. All will have their own quite distinct understanding of what it is that is prompting this urgent need to contact, to investigate, to understand.

Some will be characterised by their apparent need to acquire knowledge. Others will seek understanding, and the context of it all will be the common Quest for Wisdom and the Limitless Compassion.

Imagine, if you can, humanoid creatures from another pattern of spheres altogether, whose greater and encompassing sphere is interwoven with that greater and encompassing sphere within which Earth abides.

Imagine, if you can, the same dynamic, stirring at the heart of things, causing them also to investigate this silent and changed world of Earthly humanity. Their coming will be seen as though from another Universe altogether, and their style will be both familiar and unfamiliar, both "other" and similar. They too will respond to a loving and open heart for there is no malice in them whatsoever.

Imagine, if you can, the difficulties – even the dangers – of such incursions as we have described, for Earthly humanity is altered from its brethren and is filled with self-hatred and fear. This self-hatred and fear is projected by mortal men and women upon their fellows. How much more will it be projected upon visitors from other spheres, other Universes? It behoves all visitors to act with the utmost caution and, at the same time, to seek to reach behind the fear with gestures of reassurance, for there is nothing whatever to fear.

Imagine, if you can, an outline of possibilities such as has been suggested. The mental images will be hard to hold, the whole construction precarious. It is, however, imaginable – if only just imaginable. *Having allowed the possibility it is essential to dismantle the images, for if allowed to remain they will become ever more misleading, for they are metaphors of reality and not reality as it is.*

Nevertheless these will serve as working hypotheses, frameworks of possibility, providing a context for phenomena which would otherwise be baffling and impossible to fit into any hitherto imagined set of possibilities.

It should be noted that none of the images and suggestions presented relate to what mortal men and women might regard as the Religious Quest. No image has been suggested as to the pre-natal or post-mortem circumstances or status of human or humanoid. Attention has been focused upon the "wavelengths" and circumstances of mortal, Earthly life and that which most closely relates to it.

THE WORKINGS OF THE IMAGINATION

The images produced by the imagination must be understood as the subjective expressions of that which has been objectively perceived. To say this is by no means to deny their reality but rather to clarify their status within reality. Thus, to take an example from Holy Scripture – shared by more mortals than are likely to talk about it – a conscious, visual encounter with one of the Holy Angels will involve the construction of an image by the imagination.

The encounter with the vibrant, living being is objective; the construction of an image is its subjective counterpart. The image constructed by the imagination may display influences of Church iconography or, more probably and more truthfully, the more obscure imagery of Holy Scripture. The image constructed will be faithful but subjective, a metaphor of the reality. The objective will convey itself both through the subjective image and also in a manner which transcends it, for the subjective, on its own, is vulnerable to distortions of several kinds.

The telesmatic image, the deliberate construction of the magician, is the product of the imagination purposefully stimulated in order to construct an image which a discarnate spirit on the Earth's inner planes can use as a vehicle of communication. That this can be a hazardous procedure is not to be wondered at for it is a normal function of the imagination, set into reverse. The subjective is prior to the objective. In the normal workings of the imagination, the subjective image is the response to a prior and image-transcending objective encounter.

It is a man's imagination that interprets the everyday world about him. The more conditioned his imagination, by upbringing or by social pressures, the less he will see. He is capable of reading his own presuppositions into practically everything, and objective *seeing*, on any level, is far more difficult than might be supposed.

It is a man's imagination that interprets the inner life, not only of the world in which he lives and of which he is an integral part, but also the inner life of his own soul/psyche and spirit. Here, as never before, preconditionings and the projected fears of others can massively inhibit and distort his interpretations. It is a work of the Divine Grace in a man to cleanse, unlock, release and re-educate. Until this healing work is well in hand a man will be hard put to it either to trust his imagination or to refrain from running it wild on subjective wild goose chases.

The imagination is at once both the source of creative inspiration and the most important tool in any creative activity. In so far as the imagination is the source of creative inspiration it must be understood as a faculty belonging to the creature, Mankind, in the first instance and locally manifested in the individual. This means that it imagines what the creature, Mankind imagines, and not something else or other.

Every storyteller creates abundant inner worlds, teeming with characters. These inner worlds have landscapes and buildings; the sun shines and the wind blows, the rain falls and there is snow and ice. Trees are silhouetted against a cold moon, there are deep silences and great tumults of sound. Battles are fought, love-affairs are conducted, nations rise and fall.

Not infrequently the very characters themselves take on a semi-autonomous life of their own and tell the story to the storyteller. This is all commonplace to mortal men and women, for every child, from its earliest years, is a creator of teeming inner worlds and, as an adult, plays the same endless game but, being now adult, the inner worlds and their characters, the story and its plot can become pathological, sometimes, with tragic consequences.

This is the great work of the perpetually creating imagination. In the creation of inner worlds the creature images the Creator, for the creature is but a figment of the Uncreated Imagination and participates in its joys. There are few earthly vocations more blessed than that of the storyteller and few men or women in sadder case than those who pervert and prostitute their gift, trading integrity for advantage of worldly wealth or fleeting reputation.

The imagination is heavily involved in the interior quest of every man and woman. The art of meditation is, before all else, a prayer of the imagination whose purpose is to lead beyond the field of the imagination into the realms of the Unimaginable. On the way all manner of meditative inner journeys and invocation of archetypal forms and potencies may take place – indeed must take place – deliberately or unconsciously, for this is the way into the Silence for mortal men and women.

The imagination will enable a man to discover his own sub-personalities and to clothe them with form. In this manner they may be acknowledged, accepted and integrated, for the human condition is one of partial dis-integration. The imagination will also make a man's own interior guides known to him and, depending upon his state of inner maturity, it may clothe others, external to his own being, with form, although this must, perforce, be a more tentative and shadowy exercise.

The imagination, in short, is that faculty which introduces mortal men and women to fuller dimensions of reality, indeed to areas of their own being which were otherwise inaccessible to them. The quest must always be that for wholeness and integration. It is possible to pervert the imagination in a quest for power and advantage but that comes close to that sin against the Holy Spirit which is the final denial of truth and integrity.

The imagination will inform and prepare the mind of a mortal man or woman ahead of actual vision, be it normal or clairvoyant. The imagination will construct what can best be described as an invisible image to give substance to that which is perceived by the psychic senses, both on their natural level of operation and also upon higher levels as the natural faculties are raised and transfigured by the Divine Grace.

As mortal men and women partake of a common mind, there is commonly *known* material with which the individual imagination can work. The "conventional likenesses" of, for example, our Lord and the Mother of God, which feature in iconography of all kinds, are influenced by that which is known by the Mind of Mankind. This is not to say that these "conventional likenesses" are photographically accurate but that they convey something of a known and experienced truth of the Character behind the countenance.

The imagination constructs telesmatic images all the time, for that which is perceived by the inner senses and this is a normal operation of the human faculties and is to a considerable degree unconscious. The deliberate stimulation of the imagination to construct a form in advance for a discarnate entity to inhabit is fraught with all the possibilities of subjective projection of preconceived notions. It must be acknowledged, however, that the line between one operation of the imagination and the other can be a thin one and all encounter with non-visible intelligences of whatever kind is most safely and appropriately set within the context of deep, prayerful recollection.

The imagination is mortal man's most precious gift. Anything that stimulates the imaginative faculties of children, to the enrichment of their inner lives, is blessed and good by definition. All that inhibits the exercise of the imagination and cramps and stultifies the inner life is bad by definition. There are few words harsh enough to describe that parody of education which seeks to control the imaginative faculty, force it into "correct" channels, and attempts to condition minds to a half-life of unimaginative conformism.

THE ACCEPTANCE OF IMAGES

A man's imagination requires assistance if he is to reach beyond the bounds of his own species and into worlds quite other than that which his mortal state inhabits. Thus it is as Wordsworth perceived:

> *Our birth is but a sleep and a forgetting;*
> *The Soul that rises with us, our life's Star,*
> *Hath elsewhere had its setting*
> *And cometh from afar;*
> *Not in entire forgetfulness*
> *And not in utter nakedness*
> *But trailing clouds of glory do we come...*

But it is our common experience that:

> *Shades of the prison-house begin to close*
> *Upon the growing boy,*
> *But he beholds the light and whence it flows...*

But, sadly:

> *At length the man perceives it die away*
> *And fade into the light of common day.*

Mortal men and women have no recollection of a pre-natal state and little or no imagination of a post-mortem state either. This state of affairs is part of the human condition and, although many people come to discern that within them which suggests something "hung-over" from a former earthly life, there is no certainty. All is speculation or working hypothesis.

And yet, all is part of the common heritage of Mind, and thus, by definition, available in principle to mortal men and women. That which is known is inherently knowable but access to the limitless is limited, in this life, to a "need to know" arrangement. Thus we are protected from each other and from our own selves, lest we misuse knowledge for advantage or power.

When two worlds, two wavelengths, two sets of co-ordinates that are quite "other" to each other combine within the perception of a mortal man or woman, then the imagination must construct images to serve the commerce between them. There must be, in any event, a kind of "bridging continuum" of time-space co-ordinates between the worlds themselves. This must be matched by a "bridging continuum" of the imagination to facilitate the passages of thought between minds which are otherwise quite alien to each other.

The transmission of thought between alien minds and its translation, in both directions, into such language as the reason can comprehend – that is to say the reasoning faculties of both parties – is no simple business and must be conducted via the deep levels of Creation in which both parties find a common origin. Thus, let us suppose, a humanoid being, from a sphere interweaving with Earth, crossing from one to another within a narrow band of close wavelengths, will only succeed in communicating with a human being via their common origin at a deep level in Creation. Given willingness, deep recollection, mutual trust and a deep mutual compassion, this is possible. Once their attempts have met with a measure of success the links are formed and mind can converse with mind. Mental mechanisms will speedily manifest, in both parties, which can cause the conversation to move on from the purely intuitive to the fully rational. This presupposes, however, an uninhibited and unfearful release of the intuition within the human being so that it can do its job and provide grist for the reason's mill.

It is important to remember that all that has been described or suggested concerning the intuitive faculty and the imagination has to do with the normal equipment of a human being and its employment in certain circumstances. Lest the imagination, or the intuitive faculty, be thought to be operating in one direction only, it should be clearly understood that these faculties are as poly-dimensional as the very Universe itself.

Thus, to simplify to the point, almost, of absurdity, intuitive commerce with humanoids from other spheres might be regarded as a lateral, or horizontal, exercise of the faculties, whereas commerce with Heaven, the Saints and the Angels, might be regarded as vertical. This image, useful and mind-clearing though it may be, must not be relied upon as full and sufficient. The faculties, like the Universe, are poly-dimensional and the imagination is hard put to it to produce a model by which to interpret or understand that reality.

It were crass folly, therefore, and hugely unimaginative to boot, for a man to simply identify alien humanoids with the Holy Angels! The "who's who" of the totality of Creation is too vast to be contemplated, let alone codified and stored upon the hard disk of anybody's computer. It were better for a man, called to an intuitive awareness of other-than-the-everyday life, to take it all as he finds it without trying to be too clever by half. Knowledge is not required of him; compassion will bring a sufficiency of understanding and, if he is faithful, wisdom might yet make her home in him. **Prayerful recollection and a keen sense of humour are prerequisites for an intuitive vocation, of whatever kind.**

The establishment of an imaginative framework of understanding, however hypothetical and however obviously it is but a metaphor of a probably unimaginable reality, is prerequisite for any rational communication between human and humanoid beings from another plane of Creation. It is no less necessary that such an imaginative framework be constructed in respect of commerce between Heaven and Earth, and between the Earth of mortal men and women and its own Inner Planes, however they may be understood.

The classical construction is that of a three-tiered Universe. The Earth of mortal men and women is, as it were, the ground floor; Heaven is upstairs and Hell is in the basement! As a working hypothesis, crude though it is, it served long and still serves for multitudes of men and women. The dictum, "if it ain't bust don't fix it!" might almost be applied to it in general terms, but its inadequacies are so manifest that it must be treated with some reserve, for it altogether fails to take other than the most simplistic view of everything and it cannot fit whole fields of commonly perceived human experience into its very arbitrary frame.

Hell cannot simply be equated with the Inner Planes without both distorting, in the most arbitrary and negative fashion, interpretations of common human experience. Nor can such an equation be made without enthroning objective evil upon a throne, and within a realm, thus acknowledged as its own! This, though commonly perpetrated, is unfaithful to the Christian Revelation to a degree inconceivable, were its implications ever faced.

An over-simplistic image, however useful and – to a degree – faithful, will distort if clung to uncritically. As commerce between human and alien humanoid is not provided for within the "three-tier-Universe," the latter is in danger of arbitrary identification with Heaven (by the enthusiast) or with Hell (by the fearful). A clutch of mental images must be held together and none must be relied upon over-much for all are metaphor, all are faithful attempts by the created imagination to come to terms with that which only the Uncreated Imagination can imagine.

The images and the "inner worlds" constructed by the imagination have their own reality. By no means are they "merely imaginary" for that expression is only possible for one whose imaginative and intuitive faculties are conditioned to such a degree as almost to threaten their humanity. As all things are the construction of the Uncreated Imagination and what we call the material, physical being, is a set of energy-patterns forming pictures in the Uncreated Mind, so the creations of created imaginations partake of a similar reality but, as it were, at one remove.

The collective mind of the creature, Mankind, has an imagination of which individual persons are partakers, each contributing his or her own distinct colouring. It may be taken for granted that the collective minds of this creature, Humanoid, or of that other creature, Humanoid of another order, function in a similar fashion for they can hardly function otherwise. And as Human and Humanoid find a common origin at deep levels of Creation, their imaginations are able to relate so as to mutually construct a "bridging world" upon which, or within which, their commerce can be fulfilled.

But all is metaphor. The created imagination cannot function at the level of the Uncreated. It were faithful – and more fruitful – to accept and to rejoice than to torture the intellect with the essentially unfathomable!

COPING WITH THE IDEA OF ENCOUNTER

The context of our concern is a dynamic at the very heart of Creation. This is manifest in the growing incidence of the inexplicable within Earthly consciousness. There is a widespread incidence of encounter between human beings and apparently visiting humanoid beings from elsewhere in Creation. There is no scientifically reputable theory or explanation. There are widespread accounts of abduction, both of adults and children, in inexplicable ways, all returned unharmed.

There are accounts without number of sightings of unidentified flying objects, some of great size. There are the highly predictable signs of concern by officialdom, accompanied by denials, implausible explanations and the discrediting of witnesses. There are phenomena, such as the curiosity of the "crop circle," which cannot be rationally explained away as a prank dreamed up by two men in the bar of a public house, whatever the real explanation might prove to be.

As we are confronted by the unthinkable, the reaction of the learned tends towards a discounting of evidence, a discrediting of witnesses and a reliance upon fear and prejudice under the cover of scientific respectability and learning. This is to be expected as an initial response but, sooner or later, reality will have to be faced and working hypotheses arrived at. The currently unthinkable must become a commonplace and that which seems to threaten must be discovered to be essentially unthreatening, benevolent, and stirred by the same dynamic which is moving powerfully beneath the surface of mortal, human consciousness.

A convergence is in progress and both human and humanoid are part of it. The writer C.S.Lewis, in one of his novels, referred to the Earth as "The Silent Planet." The suggestion is here made that one part at least of the underlying dynamic at the heart of things is the restoration of that silence to harmony. The underlying Quest of all the great religions of the world has a broadly similar aim. The suggestion is therefore made that all are manifestations of the same dynamic, though there is nothing whatsoever "religious" about encounter with humanoids. Religion belongs to the human condition and is a response to its dis-integration.

In terms of the images referred to in the previous chapter, the Religious Quest of mortal men and women is primarily thought of in vertical terms. The Quest is for Heaven "upstairs" and it is conducted in some apprehension lest it end in the basement! In so far as the Quest is thought of in horizontal terms it may be summed up in the Commandment, "love thy neighbour as thyself." An enlightened mind will recognise the whole of Creation as its neighbour, but the higher and more developed religions frequently fail to match the realism of the more supposedly primitive. The North American Sioux Indian saying: *Mitakuye Oyassin* – "all my relations," which is a feature of their every religious solemnity, refers to every other created thing, animate and inanimate alike!

The suggestion is here made that an underlying dynamic at the heart of Creation is the spur both for Mankind's developing Religious Quest and also for its relentless progress in the fields of Science and Technology. That these two main thrusts are generally perceived as unconnected, if not actually at odds with each other, is but an extension of the reason-versus-intuition dis-integration of the human condition, and is thus essentially pathological.

The effects of this dis-integration are manifestly self-destructive for Mankind. Religion is turned rationalistic and loses its soul. Science, deprived of its soul, is turned soulless. The remedy is already at work within the total creature, Mankind, but its effects are yet to become everywhere apparent.

The suggestion has already been made that the irruption into mortal, human consciousness, of the alien humanoid, with or without apparent technological assistance, is a part of the same underlying dynamic which the Christian Revelation can confidently identify as Love.

Religion, as mortal men and women know it, is a product of the human condition; of that state of dis-integration which produces a sense of loss – indeed of dis-ease – in all men and women. The Quest is therefore for integration and for a restoration of contact with Reality, Meaning and very Life itself. Mortal men and women seek God, and

"God" is the name given to the Ultimate Origin, the Uncreated Mind in which all things are thoughts, the Name itself being but a metaphor, for The Mystery is unfathomable. It is, however, the experience of mortal men and women that although The Mystery can by no means whatever be *known about*, The Mystery can, nevertheless, be *known*. *The metaphor is faithful to the Reality.*

It must be one of the first reactions of any mortal man or women to project Religion upon any alien humanoid that may chance to be encountered. This, though very understandable, has within it all the potential for a disastrous misunderstanding, for the experience of quite other beings is, in fact, quite other! There may be no religious dimension to their lives in any sense that mortal men and women can recognise for – let it be emphasised – the human Religious Quest arises out of a pathological condition! It is a quest for wholeness where wholeness is known to be lacking. It is a reaction to an awareness that something is amiss.

The alien humanoid may have a wholly other experience and thus wholly other needs. The knee-jerk reaction which arbitrarily consigns to the devil any and all who do not conform to established preconceptions will undoubtedly be manifest among some of the religiously fearful. What, indeed, of the alien humanoid who "knows not the Lord Jesus?" There will be others who will make the simplistic – even crass – assumption that, as these alien brethren seem to be without religion, the existence of "God" must therefore be disproved!

It will, however, be discovered by any who have the courage to attempt such a discovery that affection and an open heart will transform any encounter. The revelation of the Christian Gospel, summed up by St John in the words: "God is Love," will find a ready echo, for it is the one truly Universal Truth.

The temptation to project the human condition upon an alien humanoid must be firmly resisted for it carries with it serious dangers for all parties. But just as the human Religious Quest must not be projected upon situations quite other than the human condition, so the human experience of scientific and technological discovery must not be similarly projected.

It must be thought possible that the scientific and technological experience of an alien humanoid could be quite other than Mankind's. The vision of such a being, and the life-experience of such a being, may well be interpreted in completely different – indeed truly alien – terms. There are no Absolutes, nor is there any limit to the number and extent of dimensions or planes of being, of "wavelengths" or indeed of anything whatsoever.

A purely intellectual approach to such problems and puzzles as may be encountered will fail. The growing weight of contradiction, paradox and apparent unreality will crush it. The intuition and the imagination will succeed, by myth, by metaphor and in the realm of poetry, where the unaided intellect must surely fail. The burden remains of seeking, with intuition and reason in as close a harmony as can be achieved, a portfolio of metaphors and of conditional mental images, the totality of which may speak an unutterable word to the depths of the being.

But it were better to accept and rejoice than to understand, for true Understanding attends that acceptance. And it were better by far to enter into an intimate *knowing* than to run the intellect to destruction in a futile, ego-driven campaign to *know about*. For it is not given to the created mind to comprehend the Uncreated, nor can a figment of the Uncreated Imagination imagine the Mind that thinks it into being.

PART TWO

"TAE SEE OORSELS AS ITHERS SEE US"

Put yourself in the place of an alien humanoid, moved by an inner compulsion that is stirring the whole of the society of which he is a part, to enter the aura of Earth and endeavour to find that to which he is able to relate. The task is daunting, perhaps more daunting at first sight than the challenge, felt by mortal men and women, to journey to the moon and to the nearest planets of the solar system as they perceive it.

Putting ourselves in the place of our humanoid brother we are bound to conclude that his vision, his perceptions both of reality and of his environment, are quite other than our own. Other they may be, superior they may not be! Our brother has a different experience of life and draws upon a different group experience at all its levels. What is unimaginable to us may be commonplace to him but, conversely, what is commonplace to us may be an astonishment and well-nigh inexplicable to him.

What is necessary, therefore, is a meeting of minds, and it is here suggested that the approach of the more mature and developed humanoid will be to establish contact, create – for his own part at least – an atmosphere of trust and confidence between himself and his contact human being, and then find ways by which each can make a beginning in the vital business of entering into each other's mind-system. The less mature and developed humanoid will be content to investigate humans and their behaviour as if they were creatures in a newly-discovered jungle or specimens in a zoo. He will be astonished and disconcerted by any such human "specimen" who requires of him a mutual interest conducted upon equal terms.

Put yourself in the place of an alien humanoid who has established a tentative relationship with a human being who has come to accept that there is neither threat nor danger in the relationship. (Other, perhaps, than from his fellow human beings who might think him mad!) The two, after brief, tentative contacts, have learned to relax in each other's presence. The human being has found himself able to cope with the situation by bestowing a name upon the alien humanoid, to whom we will now refer as "Jimmy." A bond of affection has been established between them. Our human takes pleasure in Jimmy's brief and unexpected appearances and is concerned to discover who he is, where he comes from and what he is about.

Put yourself in Jimmy's place. Here is an inhabitant of this silent sphere, similar to himself, save for his disquieting and unfamiliar appearance. The modes of perception, either of other, also seem to differ. They are existing upon slightly different "wavelengths" and thus the "reception," either of other, is somewhat fitful, although practice is enabling them (Jimmy consciously, his Earthly friend unconsciously) to arrive at a mutual "tuning" which serves quite adequately. It is hard work, however, and does not provide the inner peace and quiet which humans at least seem to need for telepathic communication. Nevertheless, these episodes are necessary preliminaries to a mutually rewarding link between mind-systems through the "exchange" afforded by an individual mind or pair of minds.

While the less mature, less developed alien humanoid is content to examine externals, rather like zoologists in the jungle, the more mature is concerned to know, understand and have compassion for *the mind*. Externals are, in any event, secondary and reflect what is within.

The link between minds, once established, obviates the necessity for actual, physical travel from one sphere to another. The topography, the environment, however fascinating, however different and however similar it might be, is but a secondary consideration. To know the mind is to know the whole person; to gain access to the Mind of Mankind is to know the species and have compassion for it and for the environment within which it lives.

Links between minds do not, however, operate in one direction only. A whole new set of dimensions, perceptions and criteria become generally available to men and women by virtue of such a link. But here a caveat must be entered, for this will be an availability *in principle;* the human condition is such that the awareness of pastures new must, for a long time, be partial, fitful and substantially inhibited.

Let us return to Jimmy and attempt to put ourselves in his position.
He has made a technological and psychological expedition of the utmost complexity and no little danger from his own sphere to that other sphere which we know as Earth. With great caution he and his colleagues have identified, and kept under observation, a possible human contact. Gradually, and very cautiously, that human being has been made aware of their presence from time to time and initial fears and suspicions have been overcome. At length, and with great apprehension, they have as it were "called upon him at home," behaving with the utmost courtesy. To their immense relief they have been welcomed with open arms and an open heart. A bond of mutual affection has been established and a willingness to help volunteered by their contact. Despite the fact that they exist on different wavelengths and have had to "tune" themselves as closely as possible, there has been a mutual awareness of near-physical contact. They are aware that they have, in a manner of speaking, "held hands." Thereafter a mutual trust is established, within the context of a growing affection and respect, and preliminary attempts at telepathic communication can take place.

All this is a thousand miles from the quasi-zoological inquisitiveness of those alien humanoids of a less mature and less developed order whose activities are frequently an embarrassment to their "elder brethren."

What are the problems that Jimmy will now face? We must begin with the assumption that a far higher degree and wider field of consciousness is enjoyed by Jimmy and his associates. We are already assuming that "he" and "him" are appropriate words to use, for we have no knowledge of the manner in which polarity is manifest in the order of being to which he belongs, nor do we know for certain if Jimmy ought more properly to be nicknamed Jemima. Let Jimmy suffice, and let him be a "he!"

His first problem may well be with our own manifestation of polarity and with the evident disorder surrounding it within the human mind. That which is fundamental, and fundamental to very Love itself, is in a measure of disarray. He will have stumbled, almost immediately, upon the first symptom of that puzzling dis-ease which has silenced the sphere, Earth, in terms of the harmony of all things. There will be whole areas of mind which will seem to be closed to him and a wholly other, wholly disturbing experience of being will present itself to his perceptions. At a kind of arms-length within his own mind he will have an experience of paranoia and be both astonished by it and deeply disturbed. In his own terms he will come to an understanding of its probable cause and it is more likely than not that his own mode of expression will be broadly translatable into a terminology more familiar to ourselves.

There will also dawn upon him that for which he was probably quite unprepared, for desperate ills call for desperate remedies and in his entry into the Mind of Man, a creature so curiously like himself but so unexpectedly tormented, he will begin to encounter the First Cause of his own being.

HUMAN, HUMANOID AND HEAVEN

The suggestion has been made that this convergence of human and humanoid, such as it has been experienced, is the product of a fundamental dynamic at the very heart of Creation. The poetry of the New Testament proclaims, "Behold, I make all things new!" and "There shall be a New Heaven and a New Earth." The suggestion is here made that the poetry gives articulation to this very fundamental dynamic. An attempt to construct a scenario for events, however tempting that may be to the human mind – which ever seeks to organize in order to control – is doomed to failure and absurdity.

A dynamic as fundamental as that which is here suggested, involving freely willed and creative creatures, some of them damaged and others possibly deviant, might be expected to require a high degree of facilitation. The suggestion is now made that the state of being and affairs which – for want of a better term – we call Heaven is that facilitating agency, transcending as it does the whole of Creation (though itself created) and participating in the thought-processes of the Eternal Mind.

Human and humanoid do not, therefore, come to an encounter unaided, though free will is at all times respected. The conduct of any such encounter is always capable of facilitation by transcending agencies if there is the humility, the simplicity, the will, to seek such aid. To state the case pictorially, with perhaps a naïve simplicity, the encounter between human and humanoid has a potential bestowed upon it by all the back-up services of the Holy Angels!

The human condition, however, makes all of this exceedingly difficult of attainment for, however enlightened an individual may become, aided by the Divine Grace working within him, society at large is at the mercy of its own deep-seated self-hatreds and paranoia. Thus the reaction to an unidentified flying object, observed on a radar screen, is to alert fighter aircraft and to attempt an interception. Official secrecy and disinformation are the taken-for-granted accompaniments to any significant incident and there is, in any event, sufficient fear of the unknown and the other-than-normal to enable any alleged witness to be discredited and the whole matter explained away in the jargon of psychology.

A more sinister trait within the disordered human psyche is that which urgently seeks to exploit any possibility of new knowledge or new and different technology and adapt it for military use. Thus one collection of human beings might be able to dominate others and, if expedient, kill them! In such a mental climate, when madness is the norm, to talk of the dialogue between human and humanoid being facilitated by the Holy Angels is to risk incarceration in an asylum for the insane. But it is the madness which is mad; it is the paranoia which is the sickness. Lies, however "official", can never be the truth, nor are they believable for longer than a very short term.

As the human condition is a sickness of the soul in which there is a derangement, a dis-integration between soul and essential spirit, the remedy is rightly described as spiritual. Human re-integration is a spiritual quest, indeed the fundamental spiritual quest in which the human soul seeks integration with its own spirit as the by-product of a reaching altogether beyond self to the Source and First Cause of all things, seeking the wholeness of re-creation.

The religious quest of mortal man and his occasional encounters with Extra-Terrestrial brethren have no obvious connection. The first may, however, enable the second to be conducted in an atmosphere of acceptance and brotherly love. The religious quest is for integration and release from paranoia. "Perfect Love casteth out fear," and fear is the great poisoner of all relationships involving mortal men and women. Religion, of itself, can swiftly degenerate into a bogus sanctification of fear, self-hatred and pious paranoia. It is Faith, and the true quest behind all the religious apparatus – sometimes facilitated by it, sometimes not – that is the thing that matters.

It is probable that a gradual human entry into the mind-system of the alien humanoid will be accompanied by a sense of absence from most of the negatives which plague the human mind. At the same time there may be another sense of the absence of several quite normal areas of mind which the human being will take for granted. By the same token, an equivalent depth of complete unfamiliarity will baffle and confuse. Only gradually will the human mind enter into these depths and only then gradually discover that which may be incomplete or dis-arrayed therein.

The meeting of minds, in a manner thus described, can only be effected if – in the language of Christian Orthodox spirituality – *the minds are located in the hearts*. Mind-in-heart can communicate with mind-in-heart; it is far more difficult, perhaps well-nigh-impossible, for mind-in-head to communicate in any depth at all.

Here again, the link between the human spiritual quest for integration and wholeness is of considerable relevance to the task of accepting, welcoming and communicating with other-than-terrestrial brethren. It is relevant as a by-product of human integration through the religious or spiritual quest.

Consciously religious or not, the quest of an individual must take him or her in search of wholeness through a gradual process of forgetfulness of self towards what a poet aptly described as "deep down things." It is an openness to "deep down things" that equips the individual to respond to an encounter with the other than terrestrial without inhibiting fear or loss of personal equilibrium.

It must now be made clear that, in this context, "deep down things" does not refer to what have been described as the "inner planes" of the Earth-state. This is very far from being an exercise in the esoteric or occult though, plainly, certain of the same modes of perception will be called into play on occasion, for not all encounter is visual by the very nature of the case.

Visual encounter, in the first instance, can be curiously inhibiting in that the senses will react to the unfamiliarity of the external instead of entering into an uninhibited person-to-person *knowing* of the essential. It tends to be the less mature, less developed among the alien humanoids who enable themselves to be seen, either physically or clairvoyantly, and thus invite interpretation of themselves and their motives from the more superficial and disordered levels of the human psyche.

Courtesy and ordinary good manners, a marked characteristic of the more mature and developed humanoid, will adopt a gradual approach by which the persons concerned come to know, trust and have affection for each other before actual sight, physical or clairvoyant, is risked. And it is always a risk, for that which is unfamiliar and different alarms. There may have to be a time of adjustment before the human contact accepts that this unfamiliar and alien-looking being is indeed the courteous, considerate and warm personality whom he or she has come to know and who has inspired no small affection through the course of their encounters.

We can only conjecture the effect that human appearance has on a humanoid, but it were wise to suppose that, having mastered something of the technique of changing wavelengths, they can see us some time before we are able to see them. They have had time, therefore, to get over the shock!

THE EXPLORATION OF INFINITY

Of necessity, we have confined our thoughts and suggestions to the Earth as it is experienced by men and women in their mortal, earthly lives. Post-mortem experience and insight must wait for its appointed time. The workings of cyclic life and being, as experienced by the other-than-terrestrial, are as yet unknown to us and are impenetrable. It is safe to assume, however, that some such cyclic life-pattern obtains and that cyclic life, in whatever form, is a universal phenomenon. All our observations of creatures, great and small, including perhaps the very Universe itself, encourage us to take such a view or, more accurately, accept such a view as a tenable working hypothesis.

We may take it, therefore, that it is with human beings in mortal, earthly life that our humanoid brethren are interested. It is necessary to state such a view because the imagination has been worked fairly hard in arriving at an image-system (however temporary, however metaphoric) which will permit the experiences of a growing number of men and women to be accommodated by the reason. We have, on an earlier page, constructed a pattern of interwoven spheres, within interwoven spheres, each sphere embracing a multitude of wavelengths, frequencies or what you will, thus enabling a near-infinity of creatures to live, move and have their being upon them (or within them).

This pattern enables the inter-sphere journeyings to be understood as possible inter-close-wavelength journeyings as well and, it is here suggested, makes the whole thing thinkable – if only just. But the images constructed are, at best, metaphors of a greater reality and must be dismantled as soon as they are made if the mind of man is not to solidify them into doctrines to disagree about.

How much more bewildering, therefore, must be the idea of quite *other*, wholly transcendent and transcending modes of being which, for want of better words to use, we are in the habit of tentatively labelling: Paradise, Nirvana, Heaven?

Once again it is necessary to dismantle images and simply to accept the wholly unimaginable without attempting to picture it, to construct forms for it, to control it.

On the basis that there is neither end nor limit to Infinity, nor yet to Eternity, simple acceptance is a reasonable option. The religious quest, in its various manifestations, contains insights into possible modes of being and becoming, both pre-natal and post-mortem. The reconciliation of these insights and the drawing out of common threads from them is not our present task. It is open to mortal men and women to deny all possibilities other than those of their current, mortal lives, but that, though probably inhibiting those lives in several respects, is irrelevant in terms of inexorable realities.

Suffice it, therefore, that a process of *becoming* is at work within the total creature, mankind, and that it manifests in and through that same *becoming* of the individual person. The realisation of the totality of human potential is the underlying intent, and that very potential is itself in process of modification to the power infinity.

It is here suggested that the Incarnation, as understood in terms of the Christian Revelation, represents a quantum leap in human potential – a leap of such proportions as to almost wholly have escaped the attention, so far, of the institutional Christian Church. The suggestion is here made that it is this infinitude of creaturely potential that may constitute the magnet which draws humanoid beings into contact with humans, though the underlying dynamic may be – and probably is – quite unconscious to both parties.

If, as the religious quest almost universally assumes, the process of becoming – of the realisation of human potential – transcends mortal earthly life, and that mankind is to be found recreated and upon a new and wholly other plane in a state to which we give the name Heaven, it is reasonable to assume that the process of becoming in other humanoid creatures will relate to the same Reality which lies behind the poetry and myth of religion. It may be that a gradual interpenetration of minds will reveal a glimmer of understanding in this respect and, needless to say, in both directions.

The experience of encounter between mortal, earthly men and women and extraterrestrial humanoids might therefore be seen as part of a wider convergence upon an unimaginable number of levels. What takes place within the *bracket of being* that we know as mortal life is that which is appropriate to that specific bracket of being. Its demands are such, in any event, as to discourage over-much speculation concerning other possible – even probable – brackets of being.

Nevertheless, that which we call Heaven is a transcendent state and manifestly – in the experience of many mortal men and women – transcends, even contains, the earthly. Thus that focus of the will upon the First Cause which we call Prayer embraces Heaven and indeed invokes it. The determined and disciplined path of the gift of self to the Ultimately Beloved raises that self, on its way, to a sufficient level of confidence and perception both to be able to take the Extra-Terrestrial humanoid in its stride and embrace him as a brother, and also to be able to respond to the help and guidance of Heaven in dealing with the situations that arise.

The whole dynamic has to do with Convergence and Becoming. It is here suggested that the words, "Behold, I make all things new," have a connotation wider and deeper than any creature can, as yet, conceive.

The realisation of potential and the coming together of what, hitherto, might be regarded as component parts of an intended whole, is perhaps that "making of all things new" of which the New Testament speaks. The canvas is too vast to contemplate, but each miniscule part of it is indeed a part of the greater whole and totally in character with it. The degree of detachment necessary to hold on to such a vision, however, is prodigious.

ACKNOWLEDGING THE MYSTERY

The idea of evolution, crystallised into doctrines of several kinds, both religious and scientific, abides within the mind of Man at the deepest of levels. Such is the human condition, however, that there is a tendency towards collisions of doctrines, with mutual exclusions, denials and negative dynamics of all sorts. It is difficult for mortal men and women to stand sufficiently far back from their own, often hasty, interpretations in order to see a wider picture and a deeper.

In religious terms there is an apparent collision between the cyclic understandings of Eastern religion and the more linear vision of the Hebrew tradition. Evolution through reincarnation, with a highly individualistic connotation, clashes with the vision of the Divine Will working itself out in human history within the context of a chosen – and representative – people. The collision is always more apparent than real for both visions are, at best, fitful and partial.

The term "evolution," in a wider sense, can be applied to the mystery and perpetual dynamic of Creation in which nothing is static, all is dynamic and all things which present to the understanding as physical are, in reality, pure energy in manifestation, the "incarnation" of ideas in the Eternal Mind. A living mind thinks perpetually, permits its thoughts to develop and changes frequently, though always in character with itself. In the context of a canvas as broad and as deep as this, man-made doctrines, interpretations of a fundamental dynamic in the created mind of Man, must sit somewhat lightly to Reality.

A human race which understands itself in terms of evolution, however profoundly that process may be misunderstood, must accept the probability that other beings, Extra-Terrestrial and humanoid, are no less subject to the same dynamic. An evolving, perpetually developing Creation is the context of all creatures and this process, although timeless and dimensionless, manifests to the consciousness of creatures in terms of time and space. The individual is thus doomed to try to comprehend the process from the wrong standpoint and in the wrong way!

By the same token, the thoughts in the Eternal Mind are timeless and dimensionless, beginningless and endless. They manifest to the consciousness of creatures as physical objects within a time-space continuum. It is impossibly difficult for the creature to accept, let alone imagine, the essentially subjective nature of phenomena, of the environment, of the very Universe, of the creature's own self.

It is difficult to grasp the idea that all that apparently exists, upon any and every dimension, plane or wavelength, is but mind-stuff, the stuff that thoughts and dreams are made of, and that the profoundest understanding of things has been articulated most faithfully by the most primitive of men; namely, that –

"There is a Dream dreaming us."

Human reason has the task of interrogating and interpreting the insights and inspirations of the intuition. When reason becomes a little god within a man and consigns the intuition to the realms of darkness, or dismisses it as "mere imagination," that man's world-view shrinks to an impossible degree; impossible in that there is no room for anything that will not fit tidily into the most cramped and miniscule field of vision. Thus rationalism is the perversion of reason, just as an irrational intuitivism is the perversion of the intuition. The role of reason is of the utmost importance for without it, in full and honest performance of its task, a man cannot function properly as a human being.

Reason must, however, acknowledge its limitations. Its function is not one of the construction of Absolutes but rather the formulation of working hypotheses. Reason must seek to establish reasonable links between its various working hypotheses and arrive at as full and detailed a picture as it is reasonable to make. One of the prime functions of reason is the making of metaphor to express that which is beyond the power of human reason to articulate or even to grasp. Reason is the maker of myth and reason is also the poet, working in close harmony with intuition, each enjoying the other's company and contribution.

The dilemma of reason is always that it is confronted by mystery, and by mysteries of The Mystery. Attempts to define mystery degenerate into lunacy if pushed too far, for mystery is, by definition, impossible of definition. Thus the defined doctrines of Holy Church must be recognized as poetry, pointing ever towards mysteries greater than they can hope to articulate, yet faithful to the inexpressible vision they seek to enshrine.

Intuition, unsupported by reason, degenerates into false mysticism and both psychic and spiritual disorder. Intuition and reason, hand in hand, mutually informing and interrogating each other, are brought into the Way of Perfection by the Divine Grace, and issue in a balanced spirituality and that genuine mysticism which is able, however fitfully, to interpret the present and passing moments of the world of time and space in terms of its context within a wider picture of the Real.

TWO TRADITIONAL WAYS

The religious quest of mortal man is his response to dis-ease and dis-integration, the origins of which are lost in The Mystery and are enshrined in human terms in a pattern of closely related myths.

The Church has constructed from this a doctrine of Original Sin which has, in many respects, become distorted and obsessional. The religious quest is inhibited and itself distorted by an excess of backward-looking speculation. It is of the first importance that the gaze be directed forward and that the process of healing and re-integration be trusted in whatever the tradition or frame of belief the religious quest is manifested.

The Incarnation (to use an inadequate but faithful term for the Christian Revelation) represents a re-creation-in-principle for the entire creature, Mankind. The Christian Church is a representative people, embracing the whole of Mankind, its every race, colour, language and tradition. The Christian Church is not a system of hierarchy, an apparatus for politico-religious power or a spiritualised dimension of a vanished imperial system. Delusions of hierarchical grandeur, or of past glories half remembered and half fantasy, notions of denominational exclusive righteousness and the consignment of nonconformists and unbelievers to perdition are grossly unbecoming, unfaithful to the Revelation and – even in worldly terms – grotesque.

The entire purpose of the Incarnation is the re-creation of the creature, Mankind, and the raising of the creature to a new and transcendent dignity. The religious quest, seen in that context, works towards the realisation, in the persons of the creature, Man, of that which is already accomplished at the heart of the total creature's being.

The suggestion is here made that, just as the Christian Church as a representative people (the yeast in the dough, as Christ describes it) exists for the purpose of helping to realise, in the circumstances of mortal, earthly life, what is already accomplished in terms of what we call Heaven; *so Mankind itself may be a Representative Creature within an unimaginable human-and-humanoid totality.*

"Behold, I make all things new," says The very Mystery's own Self: All, not just some! "There shall be a new Heaven and a new Earth."

It is almost impossible for the mortal, human mind to operate without the construction of forms. Thus, in the earlier pages of this essay, we constructed the hypothetical interweave of spheres within larger spheres, themselves interwoven, as a means whereby the mind is able to think rationally about that which is otherwise entirely baffling. This hypothetical structure was but a launch-pad and was dismantled after use. Any structure, similarly suggested, must be dismantled almost at once for, however useful a metaphor it might be in the shortest of terms, it will inhibit and mislead if allowed to remain in construction.

Our human dilemma is that *very structure itself is but a metaphor of the Real*, and that idea, though possible of acceptance, is exceedingly difficult to grasp for the simple reason that "grasping" involves "getting hold of," and there is nothing to get hold of in any normally experienced way.

The dilemma is largely resolved by the simple identification of its horns, and these can be likened to the *Via Positiva* and the *Via Negativa* as they are understood in classic Christian spirituality.

The Via Positiva, the "positive way", involves the construction of mental images, the picturing of biblical scenes, the listing and veneration of Divine attributes and the techniques of discursive meditation. It is "mental prayer" and very often, and quite properly, busily mental in that the imagination is fully exercised. This highlights the human, creaturely need for structure and indeed the human experience of structure, the time-space continuum and time as the present manifestation of timelessness.

The Via Negativa, the "negative way", involves the destruction and renunciation of all images and their treading down in a "cloud of forgetting." It involves *the Naked Intent* to plunge into the *Cloud of Unknowing* in search of God who may be known but not thought:

> *"By Love may He be gotten and holden, but by thinking, never!"*

In a balanced spirituality, the disciplines of the Via Positiva will bring the mind to a point at which all possibilities are exhausted and the Via Negativa is revealed as the only way into The Mystery. Thus Meditation leads into the Divine Darkness of Contemplation in which the darkness is the subjective response of the creature to the Uncreated Light.

It is here suggested that the parallel between the vias positiva and negativa and our need for structure in the Universe in order to be able to abandon it is a useful one.

PART THREE

THE PRACTICAL USE OF A BALANCED SPIRITUALITY

It avails nothing for a man or woman to have the profoundest insights into metaphors of The Mystery, a first-class mind, a fistful of qualifications or a position of awesome authority, unless that person is an authentic human being. Here lies the problem faced by human and humanoid alike; where is such a person to be found and by what means is authenticity arrived at? Normal, worldly criteria of academic – or sporting – excellence and impeccable conformism avail nothing whatsoever. Power corrupts and, as has been wisely observed, absolute power corrupts absolutely.

The religious quest is, at its heart, the quest for human authenticity for it is the universal instinct of mankind that the Integrity of Man is to be found in God, however the Deity is understood and whatever the mechanics propounded by a particular tradition. The Religious Institution, however, is a man-made shrine for the Divine indwelling and manifests every possibility of corruption and distortion, as history reveals and every succeeding present moment displays.

The religious quest, faithfully fulfilled in an individual, should take him (or her) through the Institution and beyond it, thereafter sitting light to it but with a limitless compassion for it, and gratitude for what it has done for him, both for good and for ill. In Christian terms, Christ is by no means limited to the institutions of the Church on Earth, nor is the Church herself confined within them. The Church is a representative people, the yeast in the dough, whose workings have to do with very Life itself. The Institutions are vulnerable to temptations to seek to imprison Life within their own-branded tin cans.

In any encounter, therefore, with Extra-Terrestrial humanoids, the spiritual quest is of great relevance. It is not a "religious" person they will seek but an authentic one; that is to say possessed of sufficient equilibrium, both to cope with an unfamiliar encounter graciously and without projecting his own imbalances and dis-ease upon them, and also to represent the human species honestly and adequately for the purpose of acquaintance. None of this has anything to do with "religion" as such, and indeed certain manifestations of "religion" would be strongly inhibiting of any such thing, but the necessary disposition may well be a by-product of the spiritual quest.

In any encounter between persons it is necessary that each should be fully open to the other. An encounter in which either one, or both, is concealed behind a "front" or an "image" is not fully human. An encounter in which the parties project their prejudices and preconceptions upon each other and never actually meet *as people* is starkly subhuman. The world is full of such encounters; they are the product of the human condition and its dis-ease, its dis-integration.

It is here suggested that, despite the dis-ease of the human condition, the circumstances of mortal, earthly life provide a unique opportunity for spiritual growth and evolution. The human experience is one of partial alienation, both from the Source and from the true self. The spiritual quest, and in particular the Incarnation which fulfils the total Quest in principle, enables every person of the creature, Man, to come to a personal knowledge of the Creator through the humanity of Christ. It is here suggested that other humanoid beings, less traumatised by alienation, may actually lack a dimension to their own spiritual awareness in comparison with fallen and redeemed humanity.

The spiritual awareness of other beings must be, and must to some extent remain, a mystery to mortal man, but without being in the least degree "admirable," mankind is nevertheless *representative*. To use the language of religion and its institutions, mortal man has a responsibility of priesthood to other beings and, as the Book of Common Prayer reminds us, the efficacy of Sacraments is unhindered by the unworthiness of the minister.

A priest is one who stands at the intersection of two worlds. He is the gate through which their commerce can take place. Christ's Humanity is the gate through which a creature can know its Creator in personal terms. The Church is the representative people for mankind as a whole. Mankind, perhaps, is the representative people for the human-humanoid totality and it is here suggested that the underlying dynamic behind the Spiritual Quest also drives the scientific quest (however blindly) and stirs Extra-Terrestrial humanoids towards this silent sphere in search of something which shall be the fulfilment of their own different yet similar being.

DIVERSITY AND PARANOIA

The possibility must be accepted that Extra-Terrestrial explorers and investigators of mortal man and his environment may come from a number of quite different starting points. These starting points may differ both in place – for a time-space continuum has to be presumed – and also in stage of development. It is here suggested that some are highly evolved and mature, others less so and inclined to be intrusive. Intrusiveness is manifested in their attitude to mortal men and women whom they might seem to regard as zoological specimens to be treated with great care and without the slightest intention to harm, but without any obvious understanding that they are dealing with such as their own selves.

The suggestion is here made that not all of the Extra-Terrestrial visiting groups are aware of the other's existence. The somewhat less mature are unaware of the existence or presence of the more mature. The latter, however, are well aware of the former. There is no rivalry or antagonism between them for they are operating on somewhat different levels and with different interests and agendas.

Others again, from outside the System within which both humans and the humanoids just mentioned abide, may or may not be aware of the others so described. The suggestion is offered that the environment of mortal man is currently popular for "tourism" of this kind and, indeed, "the environment of mortal man" is probably a better term to use than "Planet Earth" for mortal man has but the vaguest and most fitful understanding of what "Planet Earth" might mean in its totality and reality!

The scientific quest, pursued without regard for other facets of the total human quest, has produced a vast corpus of knowledge without the understanding which alone can make sense of it. A formidable task awaits mortal man if he is to integrate what he has come to know with what he is able to understand. Already the higher reaches of Physics trembles upon the frontiers of Mysticism. The "Absolute" is long discredited and the apparent behaviour of sub-atomic particles – moving through time in both directions – suggests a limitation to what can be known in intellectual terms alone.

By the same token, the religious quest, pursued in isolation, has tended towards isolated individualism and a piety at some distance from life in the market-place. The human quest has manifested all the dis-integration of the human condition and each discipline is ring-fenced against all others, with hierarchies and power structures building great empires and monuments to the ego as far as the eye can see.

The temptation must be to project such a disorder upon any alien, Extra-Terrestrial humanoid that is encountered. The "Star Wars" mentality, as enshrined in popular television and comic strip – let alone in the corridors of national and international power – manifests this to a depressing perfection. The possibility must be faced that no such degree of dis-integration obtains among our apparent visitors and that their technology (to use our own terms) is a measure of their integration. The suggestion is here made that this may be, partially at least, the reason for our own bafflement at it.

And there remains the perpetual undercurrent of "explanations," the discrediting of witnesses and, in all likelihood, official dis-information to further muddy the waters of objectivity.

The full extent of human paranoia, its fitful nature and its caprice, is probably not known to Extra-Terrestrial humanoids, for such a state of soul may be outside their own experience. The meeting of minds will reveal it – may have already partially revealed it – and their encounters with humans will therefore remain bounded by the utmost caution for some time to come. Indeed they will, for the most part, restrict themselves to a wavelength which is close enough for their own purposes but detectable to humans only via those inner perceptive gifts usually referred to as "psychic."

It will be a matter of some astonishment to them how lumbering and inefficient aircraft and other means of human transport seem to be. Their means of propulsion will seem to the Extra-Terrestrial to be well-nigh incredible and will reveal a great deal to them concerning the human race which created such artifacts.

The extent of human limitations on the one hand, and its technological achievements on the other will baffle them. Some will find it hard to believe how there can have emerged so much knowledge with so very little understanding.

And yet, there is that about the human race which draws them to us, despite hazards and that which they find inexplicable and alienating.

The conclusion may be drawn that, deep down and at the heart of things, humans and humanoids need each other. In their convergence there may emerge a greater wholeness, for "Behold, I make all things new!"

GETTING ON WITH THE JOB

The suggestion is here made that, central to the purpose of the making of all things new, is the fulfilment of the healing and re-creation of Mankind. It is proper, therefore, for mortal men and women to concentrate on the task in hand, and in particular, to the task that each individual perceives as his or her own.

The religious or spiritual quest is not to be regarded in individualistic terms. The Christian Church, for example, is a community which transcends the boundaries of earthly mortality and, as such, is both a representative people and a catalyst within the Total Creature, Mankind. Indeed the Church on Earth – which is to say in conditions of earthly mortality at any given moment – is but a fragment of the whole. It is probably the least obviously effective part of that whole! She is the hands and feet of Christ in her generation and is forever clumsy, stumbling and but fitfully coordinated, being herself immersed in the very human condition which she is there to transform.

Beyond the bounds of the wavelength of earthly mortality, healing, re-integration and re-creation are in progress and the few whose perceptions and vocations lead them to an awareness of this – and to some degree a participation in what is often a "wavelength transcending" process – bear a heavy burden of responsibility. Theirs is a calling which, given the vicissitudes of the human condition, can easily be side-tracked – even perverted – in half-unconscious ego-inflation. But dangers abound for mortal men and women and, without faith, a man would sit, housebound, fearful ever of venturing out of doors!

It is a matter of Faith that the Creature, Mankind, is healed, restored and re-created at the depths of its being by the Incarnation into the Creature of the Eternal Word of the Creator. To make such a statement is to change from prose into poetry for the realities are greater than the mind can grasp or human language articulate. What we might describe as the Cycle of Re-integration began with the Incarnation at a point in time and will be fulfilled at a point in time, yet both points are set within the context of timelessness, and there is that about the whole process which is both beginningless and endless.

Nevertheless, the daily grind continues at all its levels. Beneath it all, and indeed the context of it all, is that underlying dynamic which spurs on the gardener, the artist, the scientist, the religionist, the Extra-Terrestrial voyager and the entire dynamic of that all-transcending Reality which we know by the name of Heaven.

THE CENTRALITY OF THE IMAGINATION

One of the misfortunes of the human condition, and particularly since the Renaissance and the Reformation in the Christian West, has been the degree to which human thought has become disconnected and compartmentalised. Dis-integration is here starkly manifest and the sense of the underlying unity of things has been, if not lost, then temporarily mislaid.

The life of the imagination is threatened by the perpetual visual bombardment of television, the intuition is discounted – even denied – by excessive intellectualism, and consigned to the realms of darkness by rationalist religion. For so long has Western man in particular regarded himself as "Lord of Creation" that the commercial rape and pillage of the environment is only just beginning to be recognised as self-destructive of mortal man himself.

It is by the full and faithful use of the imagination, and an intuitive faculty released to fulfil its proper function, that mortal men and women can address the current manifestations of an underlying dynamic at the heart of Creation and make sense of them in their own times. The reason, released from its own bondage, is then free to interrogate intuition in a fully human manner. That which a compartmentalised thought-system cannot integrate becomes comprehensible, and the imagination provides points of reference that the unaided reason is quite unable to find.

All this has been suggested before in these pages but it is difficult to state it too strongly, as it is an extreme and unbalanced rationalism which blinds perception and reduces humanity to an appetite-driven, superficial cleverness. The demands of the present and future call for that true humility which is a simple acceptance of reality without projections, fantasies or fear.

IN CONCLUSION

Suggestions have been made in these pages, based upon an increasing level of human experience, which are entirely consistent with the Revelation of the New Testament concerning the Incarnation, the creation of a new Heaven and a new Earth and the making of all things new. All that is hitherto unfamiliar is the scale of the operation, the limitations – however expanded – of human perceptions of reality in the mortal, earthly condition, and the presence of untold myriads of Extra-Terrestrial brethren, moved by the same fundamental dynamic to visit, investigate and befriend their disordered brethren in this too-long-silent world.

Convergence is the word which might best describe what appears to be going on. The suggestion is here made that, just as the Hebrews of the Old Testament were a representative people through whom the Incarnation was to be effected for the sake of all mankind, so the human race (just as fallible in total as were the Hebrews) is a Representative People in whom the Incarnation is eternally effected for the sake of the totality of Creation.

The suggestion has also been made that the all-transcendent state and fellowship which we know as Heaven undergirds and facilitates the whole exercise and that unimaginable event or state of affairs which we know as the Second Coming (echoed in the expectations of all the major world religions) has a wider connotation than, perhaps, we had imagined.

But why should we be surprised?

PART FOUR

IMAGINE, IF YOU CAN, ONCE AGAIN

IT IS necessary, once again, to stimulate the imagination and to try and reach beyond our profoundly conditioned categories of thought in order to glimpse the possibilities of lives lived in circumstances quite other than our own. But again, we must beware! All that is hereafter suggested is but metaphor. No hard-and-fast theories or doctrines must be built upon such speculative foundations.

Imagine, if you can, a human/humanoid existence that is embodied and yet quite other than in the biological fashion to which we are accustomed and which is not dependent upon biological functions, as we understand them, for survival.

Imagine, if you can, a human/humanoid life in which the functions of eating, drinking and breathing have no place whatsoever, and in which life in the creature derives from, and is supported by, the total energy-field of Life itself.

This, in so far as we are able to imagine Heaven, might be suggestive of the heavenly state. But we are not talking about Heaven in this instance. It might also seem to be suggestive of a post-mortem, earthbound existence, but we are not talking of that either.

Imagine, if you can, a technology of the utmost simplicity in that it makes use of the energy-field of the whole of Creation in order to perform the functions required of it; a technology in which, perhaps, complexity and simplicity are two sides of the same coin.

Imagine, if you can, a human/humanoid life, fully embodied but, in terms of what we can only describe as "biology", quite other than our own and which is essentially androgynous. A life in which the principle of polarity, the masculine and feminine, is otherwise expressed than in the form familiar to us on Earth, and in which reproductive processes, such as they may be, are somewhat other than our own.

Imagine, if you can, a human/humanoid totality in which the abnormal are our own selves and our own biological state; in which the embodiment of the creature in animal terms is unique and completely aberrational.

Imagine, if you can, a human/humanoid totality in which one small group – our own – has fallen prey to a near-complete alienation and captivity within parameters which are fundamentally inhibiting of vision, understanding and fulfilment. In which the individual is condemned to a process of perpetual re-cycling in birth, death and re-birth, perpetually condemned to the same set of limitations and frustrations, and perpetually vaguely ill at ease with the animal in which his being finds Earthly expression.

Imagine, if you can, a state of being in which location is relatively fluid and in which mind and body are able, to some degree at least, to make themselves present for the purposes of communication with another.

Imagine, if you can, a state of heart and mind in which this natural ability is never abused and in which courtesy and the strictest respect for others prevails at all times.

Imagine, if you can, a human/humanoid totality which permits of a marked degree of difference in style, appearance and maturity; in which by no means all groups are known to all others, but in which general overall patterns of consciousness and criteria obtain.

Imagine, if you can, human/humanoid lives relating to environments which are quite other than those obtaining on Earth and experienced by men and women in their mortal, earthly lives.

Having made the effort to accept such mental images as these challenges present, it is now of the utmost importance to dismantle them and simply to accept their possibilities as metaphors of an unimagined, and as yet unimaginable reality. Above all it is necessary to accept such Extra-Terrestrial brethren as make their presences felt as if these hypothetical states of affairs did indeed obtain. It is necessary that human reason be sufficiently occupied – even satisfied in broad principle – and that the unsupported intuition be not burdened with the whole weight of experience.

The realities of which these suggestions are, perhaps, metaphors, are not in the last resort unimaginable, nor are they unreasonable only because they are unfamiliar. The totality of Creation lies within the scope of the human mind, and the image-making process is limited only by the conditionings of life-experience on Earth. There is an urgency in the process here suggested. Human and humanoid are coming increasingly in contact and the process can only accelerate. It is of the first importance that humans be found to be human and that the process of creaturely re-integration which is already in hand shall altogether transcend the demonic frustrations manifest in Star-Wars fantasy and Military and Political paranoia.

A FINAL WORD

The attempt must be made to put ourselves in the position of an Extra-Terrestrial Humanoid who, for motives but half-understood, is drawn to enter the aura of the Earth and attempt to make contact with long-lost, but never quite forgotten brethren. It is probably better to use the word "aura", despite its occult connotations, than to speak of Earth's "atmosphere" or even of its gravitational field. We are dealing with that which is *other*, and so the terminology, however vague, and even – to some – suspect, must seek to reflect that *otherness* which we cannot readily imagine.

Just as, for example, the planets Venus and Jupiter, in the Solar System as we observe and experience it, are shrouded in dense, swirling clouds, the penetration of which must be hazardous in the extreme; so may Earth itself be shrouded, but in another manner.

The suggestion is here made that, to the Extra-Terrestrial adventurer, the aura of the Earth is indeed shrouded in darkness, the penetration of which is fraught both with difficulties and a degree of hazard. The Extra-Terrestrial adventurer is entering a polluted and alien environment. The religious mythology of mankind, in many traditions, gives indications as to the origins and nature of the pollution. Let us leave the matter there. Suffice it that a degree of skill and experience may be needed for an Extra-Terrestrial to negotiate the hazards without loss of orientation, or even a measure of vital energy.

The suggestion is also made that, despite the clinging and disorientating clouds of darkness, a light shines to which the Extra-Terrestrial voyagers from various sources are drawn, as if to a magnet. This drawing, this inexorable attraction, may be variously interpreted by those so drawn. It is here suggested that the almost universal experience of those encountering Extra-Terrestrial brethren has been – however startling and bewildering – essentially benevolent. There is manifested a desire for acceptance and for friendship, and in all except the less mature and thus more intrusive species of Extra-Terrestrial, a deep and touching courtesy and respect for persons, the encounter with which can be a humbling experience for an Earthly mortal.

The Ultimate Agenda, if we may so describe it, is unknown to the many and varied participants in this activity. There is that, in mortal man, which speculates as to the possibility of Extra-Terrestrial visitants being engaged in some kind of rescue mission. Do they seek to rescue such of the human race as will pay heed from the effects of inexorable environmental catastrophe, or from the ultimate self-destroying war? There is also that, in mortal man, which projects human disintegration upon any alien visitant and can think only in terms of fear, enslavement or exploitation. That which is *other* and beyond control or manipulation is the ultimate threat to the corrupted institutions of earthly government.

The Christian Revelation enshrines an Ultimate Hope. It is articulated in terms of a Second Coming of Christ and of the final reckoning, with all that is objectively evil or malign, that will then ensue. There are echoes of this Ultimate Hope in the mythologies of other great world religions.

It is tempting to picture the Second Coming in religious terms. Heaven, as depicted by pious artists, is made to look improbably "churchy!" The Incarnation was, on one hand, an endorsement of mankind's religious instincts. On the other hand it was the fulfilment of them all. Religion is thus in a state of redundancy and the main function of the Christian Church is not the perpetuation of religion as such, but of announcing the Truth, the "good news" of Life Eternal and that the whole Character of the Ultimate Mystery is revealed in human terms as Everlasting and Unconditional Love.

Heaven, a state of being transcendent of everything with which we have been concerned, is the ultimate fulfilment both of human and humanoid, for it is here suggested that humans and humanoids alike are all *persons* of the one Creature.

The Incarnation represents the re-creation-in-principle of the total Creature, begun in mortal, earthly man by virtue both of the darkness into which earthly man had fallen and also of the essential Character of The Mystery. It is the response in Unconditional Love to the creature's calamity. It could not have been otherwise.

Heaven, a state concerning which it is easier to speculate than to imagine, is thus the guiding dynamic of all this convergent activity. Despite the ecclesiastical character of most iconography, Heaven is unlikely to be very much concerned with religion, and with *religion as such*, not at all! Heaven is Eternal Life in an unmitigated and uninhibited relationship of Love between creature and Creator – and indeed between creature and creature. Heaven is Life lived, consciously, at the Heart of The Mystery, and Heaven is The Mystery fully alive in the fulfilment of Creation.

It behoves mortal man, therefore, to relate to his Extra-Terrestrial brethren, in so far as he encounters them, as fellow-travellers in the way of Ultimate Fulfilment. Each has much to learn from the other but the underlying Truth, the fundamental dynamic behind the convergence of long separated brethren is simply this:

That in human/humanoid terms, "The Word became flesh and dwelt among us."

> Anthony Duncan
> Corbridge
> Northumberland
>
> *Feast of St Bartholomew 1996*

APPENDIX B

EDUCATIONAL EXPERIENCES

EDUCATIONAL EXPERIENCES
1. OF AN ALTERNATIVE UNIVERSE?

THE PHENOMENON
(An Educational Experience?)

How may I best approach this phenomenon? First of all, how may it best be described?

It was an unseen presence, indeed a group of unseen presences, perhaps two or three in number. They were encountered in the kitchen and in the larder of the old house and they also made their presences felt, at night, in our bedroom. I would awake and know they were there.

We were both aware of them, in our different ways. Indeed three of us encountered them. The third, taking all things of this nature in his stride, had a shadowy visual image of them within his mind which he was able to describe, casually, over the breakfast table.

Let it be said that the three of us are no strangers to the unseen presences; this kind of encounter has been part of our lives for thirty years. Indeed we have been given, each in our own way and in accordance with our needs, a measure of that discernment by which it becomes possible to know intuitively what kind of an unseen presence is impinging upon our awareness at any one time.

As a priest, this has been of great relevance to the ministries to which I have been called and, as a theological thinker, I recognize that there is a distinction to be made between the natural discernment, which is at a psychic level, and that same discernment, transformed and transfigured by Grace, by which it enters other realms which we may call the spiritual or mystical. It has been given to me to experience that quite fundamental distinction.

My own immediate instinct, in any unseen-encounter situation is to "touch home base" instantly by withdrawing, interiorly, into prayer. This has the advantage, among others, of making it clear to me whether this encounter is "my business" or "not my business." The distinction is important.

What were these presences, therefore, and from whence did they come? And what, if anything, was their business?

They were not earthbound human spirits in need of ministry and release. I am wearisomely familiar with this kind of presence, sometimes encumbered with that demonic force which they have permitted to bind them, sometimes not. No, my visitors were not ghosts.

They were not earthbound in other ways either. They were not denizens of some earthbound mini-paradise, seeking to contact and to impart esoteric wisdom to me. Nor were they those engaging inhabitants of our part of the countryside as it had once been (and, to them, apparently still was) who were as startled to encounter us as we were to encounter them.

And no! This was not Heaven impinging thus so directly upon our awarenesses. These were not the Holy Angels! Nor were they masquerading as angels of light while being something rather different. I have encountered such.

I had a strong feeling that they did not belong to any levels of our Earth-related world at all. All my inner senses seemed to support such a view. Ah! They must therefore be aliens!

A LABEL IS NOT ENOUGH!

But what is an alien? An alien is someone or some thing, who does not belong. A "foreigner." The word has become tainted by association with "enemy aliens", as unfortunates subject to a hostile government were categorised during the World Wars.

So I had foreigners in my kitchen! What kind of foreigners?

As I was aware of them it seemed reasonable to expect that they were aware of me. So I greeted them. "Peace be with you!" and "The Peace of the Lord be always with you!" There was an immediate relaxation of tension – their tension, I realised, and not only mine. Contact had been made, and on the right basis. The awareness of presence faded.

This pattern of events repeated itself several times. At night I had woken up two or three times to find their presences in the bedroom. I was now able to greet them – "Peace be with you!" – and somehow to convey to them that it was necessary for us to sleep at night!

COMMUNICATION. BUT HOW? AND WHO WERE THEY?

Communication is not a problem to my understanding. My mind has "met" others on innumerable occasions and I am quite persuaded that there is an adequate translating mechanism which can render essential meaning into comprehensible form in my own language. This has to be treated with caution because the likelihood of subjective "scrambling" is considerable. But at least the principle of the thing seems clear to me and my experiences over thirty years have tended to support the hypothesis.

That there is a bridging mechanism between "worlds" at mind level is, to me, self-evident, whatever the caution with which it has to be approached. But it also seems to me that there is also the likelihood of some kind of "bridging continuum" as between one set of time-space coordinates and another.

If the metaphor of radio wavelengths and frequencies, and indeed of the different "worlds" of television as evidenced by their different channels, is valid as a way of understanding the possible relationship between "worlds" then the occasional collision of time-space continua might be likened to the "harmonic." As a very young soldier, operating wireless in a tank, I learned how necessary it was to "net in" accurately and distinguish between being tuned in properly or being tuned in to one of a number of possible harmonics of the correct wavelength.

Were my visitors in my kitchen on a "harmonic" of some kind, to our mutual puzzlement? I think not. There was too much of an air of purpose about it.

I am quite happy, however, to attribute our occasional encounters with local aborigines of a former age to a "harmonic," as both parties were equally startled! Startled, but not frightened; an important distinction.

I became persuaded that my new acquaintances were alien. They were "foreign!" But they were peaceful, even friendly. Who were they?

WHAT KIND OF FOREIGN?

There is much speculation about visitors from "Outer Space" and there is an abundance of literature describing encounters with "flying saucers" and unidentified flying objects of many descriptions. There are accounts of encounters with humanoid beings, apparently from such craft, and even of abductions of men and women for short periods and of their detailed examination by their abductors. There is also every sign of obsessional silence and "security" by officialdom on this matter.

Let me say at once that I have no difficulty in accepting the possibility – even the probability – of there being a substantial body of truth in all this. The various "explanations" of these things are a great deal less credible than the acceptance of their essential possibility. I keep an open mind.

Were my visitors the crew of an Unidentified Flying Object? Was a Flying Saucer parked, cunningly concealed, close to the Vicarage?

I have no hesitation in dismissing any such idea. Why? An inner awareness that this is so, supported by the same awareness in the third of our number to encounter them.

Not only an inner awareness, however. The Flying Saucer type of phenomenon has to do with *a technology*. Supposing that there is a hard core of truth and reality at the midst of the "U.F.O and Alien" controversy, we appear to be encountered with beings not too unlike ourselves who are dependent upon technology in order to visit us. We are impressed by a technology we cannot yet understand.

What does this technology achieve? Does it fly from, let us say, Venus or Mars, at unimaginable speeds? Or does it, by some means, *change wavelength* and come from another, and quite invisible, environment into our own, and back again?

We don't know and it may be some time – supposing these reports to be factual – before we do know. But, however "advanced" this might seem to be, it remains very much at our level. It is a technologically-enabled intrusion, benevolent or otherwise. It is effected *from without*, it is not from within.

We project our own problems upon others and we project our own hostilities and insecurities upon everything strange or alien. Our mental images of inter-planetary travel are demonised by our obsession with "Star Wars." Being children of Adam and Eve, we take it for granted that Cain will always kill Abel. Our first instinct (faithfully manifested in our fictional literature) is to call in the military!

I am quite persuaded that my Foreign Friends were – indeed are – peaceful, benevolent and anxious to be friends. I did not project "Star Wars" upon them, nor they on me. There was, however, a slight tension in our mutual awareness until I held my arm out to them and said "Peace be with you!" At once the tension vanished, and its release was mutual.

I am also persuaded that their entry into our consciousness was not dependent upon external hardware of any description. The "technology" was interior, if such words can be used. A bridging continuum between one set of coordinates and another was established and there was a meeting, possibly less of minds than of hearts.

Remembering the definition of prayer as "standing before God with the mind in the heart," the proper basis for any meeting of minds must be, in any event, between minds-in-hearts.

STAR-WARS OR HIERARCHS?

The "U.F.O. and Star Wars" mental ambience is productive of enormous error and confusion in any approach to alien phenomena, but there is another that is, arguably, even more mischievous.

It is manifested in Esoteric Schools which are founded upon the psychically received teachings of one or other of the discarnate Gurus who are apparently concerned to illuminate mankind with their own post-mortem insights.

Anything received in such circumstances has to be examined objectively and judged on its merits. Certain it seems to be that departure from this life bestows neither omniscience nor instant Doctorates in Divinity. The mischief, however, resides mainly in the disciples, for fallen humanity has a natural obsession with hierarchies. Knowing itself to be both ignorant and highly fallible it seeks Wisdom (by which it usually means knowledge) from "higher" or "more evolved" spirits than its own.

In any Guru and Disciple relationship whatsoever, great chasms yawn to swallow the unheeding, the undiscerning and the mutual traders of personal responsibility!

I am therefore faced with the question, within myself in the first instance, "Are these presences come to teach me?" And I must also turn the question round upon itself; "Are these presences come to learn from me?" I am reluctant to believe that they are merely tourists on a day-trip. This exercise must, I believe, be to some purpose.

Am I in the presence of spirits "more evolved" than me?

I truly believe that this whole line of thought, if pursued, can end in a profounder mischief even than star-wars projection.

One dimension of star-wars projection, upon a religious rather than a military note, would be to regard this as absolutely and under every possible circumstance a deceit of the devil!

My lifetime's experience, my whole inner integrity, tells me otherwise. I will not give such honour to the evil one.

PEOPLE, NOT PLACES

Since our first encounter we have moved house. After three weeks or so in the new place I walked into the spare bedroom to find the unmistakable presences there. A happy choice of room!

Again, our greeting. Again, the relaxation of a much reduced initial tension and a fading away of the sense of presence. Contact had been established again, and again on a proper basis.

So our Friends were people-centred and not place-centred! I recalled that the third of us to encounter them had reported that one of our Friends had apparently accompanied him home to Glasgow for a brief while! We compared instincts about them.

Our instincts combined to suggest to us that these were by no means visitants from "outer space", nor were they angelic messengers, nor were they hostile, nor necessarily subject to the same problems and distortions as fallen (but redeemed) humanity. They could be described as "humanoid" – and no doubt they would describe us as "them-oid!" – and certainly relatable to ourselves. They were substantial as persons. From where did they come?

It was not difficult to accept what our instinctual voices were saying to us. They belong to a different universe. The fact that it is not, at once, possible to construct a mental image of such a state of affairs is irrelevant. The possibility is not unacceptable and the working hypothesis must be given the chance to prove itself.

It is, in any event, both the height of arrogance and the abyss of ignorance to arbitrarily deny all possibility of existence to anything we cannot either see through a microscope, or through a telescope, or take to pieces on a bench!

Allow the possibility and regard it with compassion and with interest, with the mind in the heart.

Our Friends – my wife refers to them as "our Chums" – are quite simply that. They are brethren in Creation, but we regard them as Friends, and friends stand upon an equal footing, each with something to give – and to receive – from the other. I am quite persuaded that they will come and go as our minds-in-hearts find appropriate. God bless them!

And the word that came from them, loud and clear, to my mind in my heart, was: "Convergence."

AFTER REFLECTION

I feel myself to be under a strong inner compulsion to accept, not only the possibility but the probability, that a measure of communication is established between myself and our newly encountered friends. This communicating link between minds must, I believe, operate at some higher level of the unconscious via the workings of the great Mystery of Mind of which I can know nothing.

To entertain such a possibility is to become altogether estranged from conventional, everyday ways of thinking and of understanding. The very idea does great violence to the world-views with which the majority feel comfortable. Let me therefore articulate this enormity.

I am entertaining the notion that a communication channel is in place and operative between my mind and that of one or more humanoid beings who – I presume to understand – belong not to Mars, Venus or some other part of our Solar System, even of our Universe, but of an "other" Universe altogether!

THE EVIDENT PERILS

To entertain such a notion is to risk a number of calamitous possibilities, among which can be listed gross spiritual or psychic pride, fundamental misinterpretation, delusion in any of a number of forms, and even insanity under a number of clinical labels! Any and all of these must be accepted as a possibility. Also to be accepted as a possibility is that the realities are exactly as outlined and that a communication link is in place and operative.

I have not been so insistently aware of the occasional presence of my friends for some weeks. It may be that it is not now necessary for them to be put to such trouble, nor myself to the inconvenience of dealing with the disturbance to what I will call the "psychic environment" that such a modification to the established patterns and order of things tends to provoke.

It is no longer necessary to sail the Atlantic in order to talk to an American; we now have the telephone. This metaphor is probably apt.

AN ALTERNATIVE UNIVERSE?

What do I mean by an alternative or "other" Universe? The answer must be that I don't know and am hard put to it to find an image for my imagination! I am persuaded that our Solar System, as we understand it, is only the Solar System as it exists upon our own wavelength or frequency. Change the wavelength and it will look very different – and so shall we.

I have no "world-view" difficulties in accepting the possibility that U.F.O.s exist and that they and their occupants may represent a humanoid technology which enables certain parameters of time, space and wavelength to be transcended. I can imagine such a state of affairs – just!

When I refer to an Alternative or "other" Universe, however, I do not think that I am referring to this. I am not suggesting a shape-shifting, wavelength-hopping technology from within a particular bracket of wavelengths or frequencies within our Solar System or Universe. I believe myself to be talking of something other than that – completely other. I cannot, however, imagine it.

A WORKING HYPOTHESIS?

I find myself holding on to the one word that came into my consciousness, which it may be that my mental processes received and translated into a faithful meaning. That word was "Convergence."

I therefore advance, as a working hypothesis, that my new friends and I are set upon a converging path – I will not call it a collision course – and that there may be some kind of "coming together" between their Universe and our own. It may therefore matter that there is the possibility of a meeting of minds for the benefit of both sets of parties. I will be content to leave the matter there and await developments.

A PROVISIONAL CONCLUSION

On further reflection it may be that my part in this matter is over. I am a priest, and a priest is one who stands at the intersection of two worlds; he is the door through which the two worlds conduct their mutual commerce. The humanity of Christ is, supremely and eternally, that door, and those who are in Christ are called to participate in the various aspects and functions of His High Priesthood.

Perhaps, therefore, this encounter with unexpected friends has taken place in order to establish a communication not to me, but rather through that priesthood in which it is my vocation to participate. This were by far the better thing, for it calls only for an open heart, an open mind and open arms. Given these, the door stands wide and welcoming. I stand in detachment from the process and cannot – must not – run about after it or in search of it or I desert my post. I am thus released from the grosser possibilities of ego-inflation, distortion and delusion.

I am thus very well content to leave the matter there.

13th October 1995

2. FROM ELSEWHERE WITHIN THIS UNIVERSE?

THE PHENOMENON

SOME two or three years ago we became aware of being "visited" in some way, usually at night, by persons who we came to understand as alien to our own Earth and humanity. They were not visible but their presence was sensed psychically.

Following upon one such visitation, at night, Helga had occasion to visit the bathroom, and both on her way there and on her way back, she became aware of a soft but unmistakable hum, as of an electrical transformer, coming from just outside the house, in or very close to the stable yard. Nothing was visible but something was unmistakably "there."

Within the last week or so this phenomenon has reoccurred at our new address. I woke up, suddenly and with total wakefulness, to a strong sense of "presence." At the same time I became aware of a soft but unmistakable humming sound, coming – as it seemed – from the bay window of the bedroom. It was as if the unseen source of the sound was half in and half out of the room.

After a few moments the sound altered as if its source had increased power and "lifted off." The sound became steadily more distant and then ceased. At the same time I became aware that the sense of "presence" had also ceased.

One or two evenings later – it may have been the next day – we were reading and watching TV in the drawing-room. We both heard the dining-room door, behind the dividing curtain between the rooms, twice give a sound as if something was pushing upon it. The door is inclined to stick and sometimes releases tensions caused by pressure during the closing of it and so we did not take too much notice at the time.

A little later, however, something caused me to investigate, and on opening the door into the hall, I was confronted both with an almost overpowering sense of "presence" and a great sense of tension. This was evidently a Visitation of some consequence.

I said "Peace be with you!" and, in prayer, was told who they were and what I must do. I greeted them in the Name of our Lord and of the Holy Trinity, I welcomed them and accepted them and said that, whatever the Will of God for us both was, I would work with them. I say "them" because there seemed to be a group present rather than an individual.

There was an immediate relaxation of tension. I realised that they had been quite apprehensive as to my reaction to them. We were now, quite evidently, friends. I returned to watching TV and told Helga all about it. She was not particularly surprised.

A half-hour or so later there was a loud knock on the dining-room door. I opened it and encountered the "presences" again. I was puzzled by this and sought, in prayer, an indication of what I should do. I was told that they were waiting to be invited to depart! Good manners! I greeted them again and bade them farewell for the time being. The "presences" then faded from my consciousness.

I was given to understand that they belong to the same Universe as we do, that they might be described as humanoid but are better understood as Elementals of their own place than as Human in the way we are on Earth. I was given to understand that clairvoyant vision would have seen them clearly (I am very seldom clairvoyant) and that they may well become visible to me in due course and that their appearance would occasion me no alarm if they did!

This seems to be a "gateway" exercise as far as I am concerned and I await developments. I make no speculation as to the cause or nature of the electric-sounding hum.

◊

Subsequently, our sleep was disturbed, some nights later, by the arrival of a somewhat different set of visitors who, I sensed and was then told in prayer, were not the same and came from elsewhere in our Universe. I was told to greet them and then ask them to leave as this was the time for our rest! I gathered that they had also been to see us before but were not, at the moment, really our business to deal with.

2nd December 1995

3. A MUTUAL ATTEMPT AT COMMUNICATION

24th April 1996
Since our arrival in Corbridge, and particularly during the months November and December 1995, and at intervals afterwards, we have been visited by what I have come to understand as no less than four different groups of non-terrestrial persons.

Some we had begun to encounter already at Whitley Mill; these included a group of tall, solemn beings whom we were given to understand belonged to a different Universe altogether. They have visited us at Corbridge occasionally and there seems to be a friendly, even affectionate "rapport" between us. They are somewhat remote, however, and rational communication has not yet been accomplished or even seriously attempted.

Three groups of Extra-Terrestrials have impinged upon our lives. The first (the *1st xi*) seem to be about six feet in height and highly developed in all respects. With these, a real bond of affection has been established. I am pleased to see them.

A second group (*2nd xi*) seem less highly evolved, and they seem somewhat shorter, perhaps four feet to four foot six inches in height. Whereas the words "wisdom and understanding" spring to mind with the first group, the word "knowledge" seems to characterise the second.

The *2nd xi* are inquisitive – occasionally intrusive – and are inclined to regard us as "species" to be investigated. It has been necessary to make it clear to this group that I will be treated by them on equal terms or not at all! This caused them evident consternation and they have not returned since.

A third group, altogether more primitive, (the *"A" xi*) had to be firmly but kindly told to leave – albeit with a blessing!

I am inclined to think that technology of some kind may be involved in the appearance here of some or all of these groups, and this might have a bearing on the many, and differing, accounts of U.F.O.s and their alleged inhabitants. But this is speculation on my part, I do not know.

It appears that the *1st xi* are aware of the others – and appear almost embarrassed by their activities – but the other two groups are unaware either of the *1st xi* or even, very clearly, of each other. I offer no explanations or theories, this is simply as it has come to my understanding.

A few days ago, the apparent leader of the *1st xi* group – whom I have named, affectionately, Jimmy, arrived and managed to make me understand that they would be making an attempt to communicate rationally with me. There had seemed to be some kind of an attempt before but of no consequence in terms of content.

Yesterday I was warned, while at prayer, that I was to be ready, seated in my chair at 10am, with a pad and pencil. The attempt would be made by telepathy and there was no need for the actual presence of the communicator in the room.

Imagine, if you can, a corduroy-and-sweater-clad figure seated in an armchair with his angel guardian standing (figuratively speaking) by his shoulder. After prayer and recollection the transmissions began, the angel prompting and guiding. Here is the transcript:

Me: Peace be with you.

X: Peace be with you.

Me: What are you trying to do? *(I was dissuaded from asking either "Who are you?" or "What do you want?")*

X: Unite with you.

Me: What do you mean by that?

X: That we become one.

Me: Why do you wish to become one with us?

X: The time has come.

Me: How do you wish to become one with us?

X: In love and friendship.

Me: Do you know that we are a damaged people?

X: Yes, we do.

Me: Does that make you cautious?

X: Yes, it does.

Me: How can I help you?

X: Do you wish to help us?

Me: I wish to do the will of the Love which created us both.

X: Will you take us into your heart?

Me: Very gladly, the Lord being my helper.

X: Who is the Lord?

Me: The Love which created us became one of us, suffered all the effects of our damaged state and rescued us. He is the Lord.

X: That is beyond our experience, but we accept.

Me: The peace of the Lord be always with you.

X: Thank you.

Me: God bless you.

X: That is our wish for you.

Here the communication ended. Its mechanics were quite simple; I "thought" a question (or a reply) at the mental blank within which, or beyond which, my colleague was situated. The reply (or a question) then flashed into my mind. Sometimes there was an interval at both locations as if consideration, or guidance, was given as to what to say next. If in doubt (which was seldom) I checked with my angel guardian. Once he had to prompt me to write a reply down because I was on the point of dismissing it as entirely subjective – which it was not!

A high level of trust is necessary for this kind of thing, and a great deal of faith in the essential possibility of the transmission of meaning telepathically and its rendition into language. I have no difficulties with the idea and none whatever with the realities of telepathy on all kinds of levels.

It is not, however, to be played with or used lightly, but only prayerfully and under obedience. It is, needless to say, vulnerable to all kinds of subjective manipulation and delusion.

I had asked my angel guardian before we began: "Do they know Jesus Christ?" The answer was both yes and no, their experience in

Creation is other than our own; they know that which is right and appropriate to their case. "Do they know Heaven?" I asked, meaning the fellowship of the Angels and the Saints. "Very much as you do, but differently," was the answer.

The impression I am left with is that these good folk have not suffered the same trauma as the Human Race and that which we call "original sin" and all its ramifications has not been their experience, though doubtless they may well have their own problems and resolutions.

Simply stated, I am left with a kindly and affectionate impression of persons with whom we can "do business." I hope with mutual blessings and benefits, and above all, to the Glory of God.

And I have become very fond of Jimmy!

Lightning Source UK Ltd.
Milton Keynes UK
UKHW012352060622
404005UK00001B/170